'As an experien . But this book gave me a my voice and my messag relatable case studies, an rt Bewley has written a book that everyone who speaks in front of an audience of any size – from 10 to 10,000 – must read!'
Jeremy Neuner, Founder and CEO, NextSpace, TEDx Speaker, Startup Program Manager, Google

'This is a "must read" for anyone who wants to be a better presenter. I started reading it and couldn't stop – it is full of practical steps that everyone can use to transform their approach, build their confidence and become a compelling storyteller.'
Steve Pierce, Deputy Managing Director and Chief HR Officer, Hitachi Europe

'Storytelling is the magic ingredient that makes you stand out when bringing your message across. If you are looking for a guide that combines theory with hands-on exercises, this is the perfect companion!'
Christian Schmeichel, SVP and Chief Future of Work Officer, SAP

'Your story makes or breaks your success. I have seen this in the last 25 years in startups, large corporations and with myself. I have been lucky to witness the amazing impact of Stewart's work both with startups and with myself over the

last five years. It is exciting to have him bottled in a book. This book will help you mint your story and break the invisible barriers that are strong and real.'
Francisco Lorca, Founder & CEO, EthosData, Board Director, MoneyGram International (NAS:MGI).

'As someone who is not a natural public speaker but has to present for a living, and who'd love to tell better stories, this short and practical book is a game changer. I feel coached.'
Audrey Tambudzai, TEDx Speaker/Contributor, CSW65 & 66 UN Women UK Delegate, Strategy Consultant at Anthesis Group

'I have known Stewart for almost a decade and seen him coach many, many startups (including a fair few I have invested in). As a venture capitalist, all I ever want to hear is the founder behind the jargon, and Stewart has an uncanny ability to unlock their story. Now he has written down all his secrets into a really practical guide that could help you unlock that next funding round, get that promotion or simply unlock your inner voice.'
Jon Bradford, Dynamo Ventures

'In a world of often compelling but rarely practical business books, Stewart's *Speak!* achieves both. It's compelling in the way he weaves his own personal stories and examples with those of the clients he has coached over the years. And it's highly practical because every chapter – or act – includes practical tips, tools and exercises that put the theory or principle into practice. From knowing and tackling your gremlins to standing tall and using your voice, mastering the art of storytelling to taming your adrenaline and overcoming your fears, this book is crammed full of entertaining and – from my own personal experience – effective ways to make any presenter better. Whether you're preparing to present something for the first time or you're a seasoned TED Talker, there will be something in Stewart's guide for you. It won't be long before *Speak!* is a well-worn, liberally dog-eared staple on my bookshelf, to be sure.'

Nigel Miller, Senior Advisor, Culture and Talent, Edelman

The advice in this book transformed my life and helped me realise I had a story people actually wanted to hear. I have now told that story over and over to many rooms full of people. The simple, broken story Stewart helped me release led to me starting a national mental health charity that is growing daily – all because I stopped apologising for my voice and slayed a few dragons. This book is a gem for all with a story to tell – and that means everyone. It is inspirational but also extremely practical. I am so glad Stewart has made this great journey available to so many. Get it, read it, do it... And along with me, I hope your story will make a difference to many – as you stop simply talking and learn to really speak!'

Ruth Rice, Founder and National Director, Renew Wellbeing

'Stewart is a master at getting anyone to unlock their voices. It isn't magic (even though sometimes you feel it is). There is a deliberate process and I am so grateful that he has laid out his secret sauce in this book. It is never as good as the real thing – so after you have read it, book him!'

Christer Hollman, Founder, Divido

'I have worked with Stewart for over ten years now, and he is, without doubt, the best pitch and storytelling coach there is. His new book *Speak!* is a brilliant – and super practical – guide to the art of storytelling and how you can defeat your demons to unleash the storytelling hero within.'

Ben Mumby-Croft, Director of Entrepreneurship, Imperial College London

STEWART BEWLEY

SPEAK!

BECOME A STORYTELLING HERO IN FIVE ACTS

amplify

Published by Amplify Presentations Ltd

Amplify Presentations Ltd is a company registered in England, no. 08534525.

www.amplify.me.uk

Cover design: Simon Baker for Thirteen Creative
Typeset by Thirteen Creative

Printed in the United Kingdom

ISBN: 978-1-7396118-0-4
eISBN: 978-1-7396118-1-1

CONTENTS

For Liz, Nate and Jessie: I love you more than words can ever say.

PROLOGUE

I founded Amplify back in April 2011 because of my friend Mia. I had been acting for years, but when Mia asked me to help her speak in public I didn't know if I could. I asked her to show me her speech so she opened her mouth, swallowed some air… and nothing came out. She had truly lost her voice, and her confidence. I didn't really know what to do. Was the approach that I used for presenting on stage as an actor applicable here? It was all I had, so we gave it a go.

I began to introduce Mia to the techniques that have proven so powerfully effective for me over the years – techniques that you will discover over the following pages. I got her standing tall, breathing correctly and connecting her voice. Twenty minutes later I had a different woman standing in front of me, speaking with confidence and commanding the space with a transformed story!

She went on a profound journey.

And it was transformative for me too. Over the past decade, this journey has led to me coaching 13,000 people in 64 different countries to become champions at public speaking. The aim of this book is to guide you along this same path to becoming a true storytelling hero.

I first met Kumi back in 2013. She was in her mid-twenties and working for a global financial institution full of strong-willed men. She didn't feel her voice was relevant, but she wanted it to be. After a few coaching sessions, she went from being a shy and polite Japanese woman whose story was easy to forget, to a strong and feisty business woman. In her last session, she told me two things.

1. She had received a phone call from her boss in New York saying, 'Kumi, people are talking about you!' This had never happened before. She had dared to share her opinion on all the calls with her seniors *and* to project her voice.
2. She had disagreed with her New York line manager on the phone a few days later and changed the manager's mind. This was also a first!

I believe in transformation – I witnessed it with Mia and Kumi. I believe in coaching people into confidence, exposing the bad habits, and giving them tools to learn great habits to unlock their voices. If you can unlock your voice you can unlock your stories and you can learn to speak with power.

We all know what makes a great story and it plays out in Hollywood movies again and again: a hero goes on a mission to achieve seemingly impossible goals, slaying literal or metaphorical dragons along the way. Inevitably, they need a wise mentor to help them succeed (often in the form of Morgan Freeman, it seems). What we don't always realise is that to become a great storyteller we need to slay our own dragons first – dragons like fear and adrenaline. And we all need a wise mentor to help us do that.

Throughout this book, that's the role I will play in your journey – if you're up for it!

That is what I do for a day job and I love nothing more than seeing people unlock their voices and hearing their stories get told. We all have a story inside of us. As we travel through the pages of this book together, I will lead you not on a Hollywood Hero's Journey[1] but on your own Hero's Journey. You will be invited to leave the old familiar territory of average storytelling to achieve goals that seemed out of reach, to discover your inner strengths, to slay the dragon of fear, to channel adrenaline and to emerge from the battle as a true storytelling hero!

If it all sounds a bit dramatic, that's because it is.

I have split this book into five acts, according to the Hero's Journey:

Act I – The Beginning
Act II – Leaping Off the Cliff
Act III – Approaching the Dragon
Act IV – The Road Back
Act V – Resurrection

I will guide you through each of these acts, both when it feels easy and when it gets hard. Consider me a Sherpa, dedicated to the task of getting you to the summit of Mount Everest.

We can do it. We *will* do it! And along the way, you will meet others who have travelled this road before you – clients I have coached through their own Hero's Journey. Their stories are in here so that you can see how they reached their heroic status. It may just be the key you need to unlock your own voice.

By the end of this book you will have taken your brand new skill of storytelling and applied it to your specific context: the business presentation that looms on the horizon, the promotion you are pitching for, the proposal you are about to make.

Science tells us that the best way to remember is to use good old fashioned pen and paper. I have left spaces on the page for you to write down your story. There are also links to digital resources scattered throughout book which will help you go deeper, including my online coaching PocketCoach Global.

Are you ready? Let the adventure begin.

ACT I

THE BEGINNING

SCENE 1

STORYTELLING. IT'S A POWERFUL THING.

Storytelling is one of the most personal and powerful things we can do.

You know this. It's why you picked up this book.

Brené Brown says that storytelling is 'data with a soul.'[2] I love sharing this with my clients who generally think that data is boring. Whether you are a data analyst, high school teacher or startup founder, pretty much anyone, anywhere on the planet agrees that stories are powerful – but so much of it is in the telling.

So many times, our presentations get lost in translation. We think someone has heard us but their takeaway has actually been something completely different. Or worse, behind their earnest nodding, they have already switched off and are secretly thinking about lunch (poached eggs and smashed avocado on sourdough does it for me...).

I bet that you didn't wake up this morning saying to yourself, 'Today I want to be really boring and totally forgettable.' And yet most presentations end up that way. Why is that? Do we just have to accept that some people are great at presenting and some are not? I don't think so. I genuinely believe that anyone can be a great presenter by learning to be a great storyteller. (Unless, that is, they don't want to be. Or unless they think they are already brilliant and don't need any help!)

What if people could actually hear what you wanted to say? What if you could take a template, something that I have seen work time and time again with my clients, and apply it to every presentation, conversation and encounter?

Because a presentation doesn't just mean a meaty, 20-minute TED talk. It might be the 30-second introduction to a meeting, the three-minute update, the snatched conversation in a corridor, the job interview... In fact, it's every time you open your mouth to try and persuade anyone of anything. And the key to an unforgettable presentation is storytelling.

Great storytelling is a lifelong skill, from business meetings to initiating new relationships, from having drinks in a pub to standing in line at a barbecue. And telling stories well is what makes life more memorable. In *Time and How to Spend It*,

James Wallman spends an entire chapter talking about the psychological importance of stories. He argues that the telling of stories is not a nice-to-have, but is critical for our happiness, because stories provide unity, purpose and meaning.

This is incredible.

Hands up if you would like more unity, purpose and meaning?

So, as we embark on the journey of storytelling, of creating and delivering presentations that make a difference, here are two things that I want you to tattoo to your hands and your forehead:

- A story is *22 times more memorable* than a fact.[3]
- The brain is wired to process *two thirds of all the information it ever receives* in picture.[4]

You have picked up this book because you want to be able to present better than you do right now. You may have a particular presentation coming up, or you may simply be deeply aware that the only way to get people to listen to you is to learn to speak really, really well. I can get you there, but it will take more than the act of just making it to the end of this book. It will require a *doing*. I am going to give you some exercises to do and we are going to use your story as a template.

Let me assure you from the start, I understand the journey you are about to go on and the moments where you will want to give up. I've been there – literally. Every exercise I ask you to try, I have done myself and have conducted with thousands of others. I will guide you through all the obstacles you will face in your quest to become the storytelling hero you never thought you could be.

So as I invite you to leave your familiar world of average presentations and set out on a quest for storytelling greatness, I would like to share with you my own journey – the tale of how I got here, to my promised land of storytelling.

MY STORY

The story I am about to tell you comes straight from my gut. It is a story I share with my clients when I coach them and I have been sharing it for the past 10 years. When Covid hit and it wasn't possible to be in a room together, I created a video of my story. You can watch it by scanning the QR code below. Whenever I share this, I emphasise different elements for different audiences but the essence is always the same. I should warn you that it is real and emotional.

WATCH MY STORY
AMPLIFY.ME.UK/STEW-STORY

I grew up in Manchester and went to a private all-boys school – one of the best in the country, apparently (according to the league tables anyway). But I couldn't play football, or rugby, and from pretty much day one I was bullied. It started out physical and then turned verbal. Maybe it was because I didn't have the physicality to stand my ground or the words to fight back – either way, I was an easy target.

When I was 13, I auditioned for a TV show and to my complete surprise I got in. But the bullying had been so bad that I approached my new form teacher in the September before filming was due to start and said:

'Mr. Stubbs, I have just got into a TV show. It means I'll be out of school quite a bit this term. Please don't tell anyone in the form because it will be really difficult for me if everyone knows. I've already been bullied and I would rather no-one knew.'

Mr. Stubbs nodded, stood up from his chair, cleared his throat and said, 'Stewart – stand here.' I stood on the small platform at the front of class thinking, surely he won't say anything? And then I heard these words: 'Boys, Stewart here has got into a TV show so he won't be at school much this term.'

It was the nail in the coffin.

My life in school was over.

The bullying got really intense the minute the TV show came out. People I didn't know would stop me in the corridor saying things like, 'You can't act.' Or even, 'I've shagged your mum.' All the usual stuff from a boys' private school, brimming with testosterone. But it got so bad that I remember being shouted out of classrooms every day at lunch. Boys would literally not stop shouting until I left my own form room, or any other room. I remember wandering the halls on my own, trying to find somewhere I could just breathe. I found it in the toilets and with the cleaners. They were kind. They didn't shout at me or bring my mum into it. They seemed to like me. And to find me funny.

Maybe that was all I needed to keep going, because somehow I did. I kept acting. I'd lost my voice, my ability to be strong with my peers, but I found it in playing parts and I found it in delivering speeches in assembly. And despite the horrendous bullying that I endured for many, many years, I found myself on the stage at the age of 18, in the Memorial Hall, giving an assembly to over 600 pupils.

I remember walking through a sea of navy blue uniforms as I made my way up to the stage. There was a wooden throne behind me and an enormous organ over to the left. I stood in front of the school and for 20 minutes I told the story of how I had been treated. I said I didn't need their pity but they needed to know that they were arrogant.

I ended the assembly by saying this: 'There's a quote in the High Master's office by Aristotle, written in gold leaf on the wall. And it says this, "We are what we repeatedly do. Excellence, therefore, is not an act but a habit."'

I said, 'I think we should change that to: "We are what we repeatedly do. Arrogance, therefore, is not an act but a habit." Thank you very much.'

I sat down expecting boos. What I got was thunderous applause. My Religious Studies teacher had her hands above her head and would not stop clapping. No-one stopped clapping. The Middle School Master got up to end the assembly, looked at the faces of the boys, listened to the sound of the applause and sat back down. It was utterly astonishing. And in those minutes that felt like forever, I didn't fully realise that I had found my voice again.

Fast forward to 2011. I'd been acting professionally for ten years. My friend Mia asked me to help her present a talk, and I thought, 'Well, I'll have a go.' She was so nervous that when she spoke literally nothing came out. She lost her voice. It was pretty extreme. I gave her a couple of exercises on how to stand tall, and breathe, and project her voice.

And her voice exploded.

Mia got her voice back. And that's when Amplify, my business, started.

It's now 2022. I've helped 13,000 people tell their stories. I've travelled around the globe (when that was allowed!) and I've worked for some of the top companies in the world.

But the truth is, it's not about the names.

Success is about being present to the people in front of me. And every time I get to coach someone now – over Zoom or over Teams or in person – I find another piece of another person's story put back together, and that's another part of my healing and my living out, helping me unlock my voice and helping others unlock theirs.

So that's my story, in two and a half minutes. It's emotional. It's real. It's raw. And it's why I am here today. When I share this in the room it gives people permission to share their own stories. If I can do it, then they can do it. If I can set the tone for what is required of great storytelling, then they can reach for that standard. Now it's your turn – let's get going on your journey to becoming a storytelling hero!

SCENE 2

SPEAKING IN SHORT SENTENCES

Daniel Kahneman won a Nobel Prize for his work on behavioural economics – how the brain works. He knows his stuff. He has discovered that when we speak in long sentences our audiences don't trust us. But when we speak in short, sharp sentences, we are seen as trustworthy.

That is not how the world speaks. Experience tells me that whether you are the CEO of a multinational corporation or heading up a brand new startup, delivering short sentences that pack in all the vital information may not come naturally to you.

You will hear me say this a lot, but the body remembers. The word for this is 'proprioception' – muscle memory. This is ideal if you happen to be an athlete, but it works against us when it comes to our bad storytelling habits. Your body has remembered to do what you have always done when you present, whether it's long sentences, or mumbling, or not looking at the audience. You will inevitably have honed some bad habits over the years.

So the plan right now is to create another habit, a good habit, and then allow our bodies to inhabit that habit! We are going to speak in short, sharp sentences and you are going to remember how it feels, creating a new muscle memory in the process.

If you can sense it, you can repeat it.

If you can repeat it, this can be your new standard for your sentences.

If everyone spoke in short, sharp sentences life would be a little bit easier – it would make meetings more pacey and engaging anyway! The smallest change can make the biggest difference and if you can simply change your sentence length you will see transformation.

I have seen it time and time again. Trust me: it works.

PRESENT TENSE

Most presenters have a head full of thoughts and desperately try to cram them all into one long sentence. But if you take us step by step, with short sentences, a certain storytelling logic occurs. Let me give you an example.

There are two ways that I can describe my Thursday morning last week. Here is the first way:

We got up late, I took my son to school, the traffic was bad, I went to the gym, came back and switched on the computer at 11.00am.

You're bored. Because it's boring. It's long and reads like a shopping list. I'm now going to tell the same story, but in the present tense.

It's 8.04am in the morning. We are racing through the back streets of St Albans to get my son to school on time. On my way home, I am determined to get a swim in before work. I am swimming my first length when I see a lot of legs appear to my left and right. I lift my head up, two lengths into my swim, and realise I am the only one in the pool under the age of 50. I am in the middle of the aqua aerobics class!

Which one is more engaging? Which one can you picture in your mind's eye? In the second version I placed myself in the present and told it as it happened. As I did this, my sentences naturally became shorter. It also prompted me to remember certain details, and it's the details that make a story interesting. Think back to your weekend. If you were to re-tell it using the present tense, what would you say? Have a look at the table below. On the left is the 'shopping list' approach. On the right are examples of how the story can be transformed by speaking in the present tense.

What you did at the weekend:	**In the present tense:**
I went to…	It's Saturday and I'm heading to…
I met my family for a walk in the park.	It's midday and I'm in the park. It's pouring down with rain and I can see my dad coming towards me wearing only a t-shirt!
We had lunch in a new Italian.	A brand new Italian has just opened on the high street. We decide to take shelter and order pizza.
In the evening we had leftovers in front of the TV.	We light the fire later on, put on our pyjamas, tuck into the homemade veggie chilli from last night and watch the second half of *Jerry Maguire*.

Have a go at putting your weekend into the present tense using the table below and on the next page. On the left create the 'shopping list' version, and on the right build it up in the present tense. Don't worry about whether you're getting this exercise 'right', or how well you're doing – the most important thing is that you do it. You are *behaving* your way into detail and into short, engaging sentences. You are starting to build a new habit. This is where the transformation begins and your audiences will thank you for taking these first steps.

What you did at the weekend:	In the present tense:

What you did at the weekend:	In the present tense:

SCENE 3

ENTER THE GREMLIN

At some point in any Hollywood movie the hero or heroine says, 'No, I can't do this.' In *The Lord Of The Rings*, Frodo doesn't want to take the ring. In *The Matrix*, Neo refuses to follow Morpheus' voice. Luke Skywalker, Katniss Everdeen... They all doubt their skill. They all feel unworthy. They all have a moment when they don't think they can do it. In other words, they all fall prisoner to their gremlins. They need a wise mentor to open their eyes to the lies they have believed, so they can realise their inner strength and become the hero they need to be.

And it's just the same with storytelling.

We think our story isn't good enough, or powerful enough, or we compare ourselves. And comparison is the killer of storytelling. You can't afford to compare yourself with others because comparison is like a fog – you can't see more than a few feet in front of your face and you definitely can't tell the difference between lack of skill and sabotage. It's my job to reveal the self-sabotage and then to give you the skills to become a storytelling hero.

Back in World War II, pilots used the phrase 'gremlins' to describe invisible things that sabotaged their plane engines. These phantom gremlins were the enemy as much as the physical enemy. So when Roald Dahl, who was one of those pilots in the Air Force, turned to writing, his first book was named *The Gremlins* – giving us a very useful word.

So we are going to name our gremlins right now – these seemingly invisible critters that sabotage our ability to tell our stories. We all have at least one. Mine is called Ken. Ken appears just as I prepare to speak, or re-appears when I am half way through a coaching session. He has three killer statements he likes to whisper in my ear:

- **Accusation 1:** 'Calm down – you're over the top.'
- **Accusation 2:** 'Why do you think you're important? That is so arrogant.'
- **Accusation 3:** 'What you do doesn't change the world, so why bother?'

If I listen to Ken, he will confirm my worst fears and the judgements I proclaim against myself. These fears will become behaviours. If I feel I am over the top I will lose confidence, second-guess myself and become a shadow of the coach I could be in that moment. If I feel that I don't add value to the room, I will speak in a way that tries to win people's approval and prove that value. If I believe that nothing I do changes anything, I will lose motivation, retreat from the room and be average.

But if I name the gremlin, call Ken out, and write down the things he says to me, then I am shining a light on a dark place. Then I can look objectively at these accusations and I can bring change. To me first. To my audience second.

So right now I want you to name your gremlin. Write the name on the page.

Gremlin name:

....

Now it's time to write down three accusations that they confront you with regularly (look back at mine if it helps).

Accusations often come as a whisper, a very politely-delivered sentence over a cup of tea. Often the gremlins come to take a seat at your table, interrupt your dinner, eat your food and then leave, making sure you pick up the bill but are left feeling empty. Their accusations and questions are a perfect combination, designed to kill your confidence and bring you down.

Accusation 1:

....

....

Accusation 2:

....

....

Accusation 3:

....

....

You did it. You named your gremlin and wrote down their accusations! This is no small thing, because your gremlin may have been hiding and whispering to you for years and years. Now they have been exposed. This is very, very powerful.

As you are grappling with your gremlin, it is so important to know that you are not alone. Over the course of this book I am going to introduce you to some seasoned travellers, who now walk with a confident stride and a glint in their eyes. They have fought their own battles with their gremlins – and triumphed. They have gone before you and are here to inspire you.

THE STORYTELLING HEROES

My business, Amplify, exists because of people. I have not stopped at simply being amazed and standing in awe of what actually happens to my clients as they unlock their story. If I could bottle the confidence that comes out of people, I would. But I can't. I can, however, tell their stories about how they learnt to speak. And my hope is that, as you read these stories, you will be able to see your own story in theirs. If you can, you will start to see yourself as a storytelling hero, too. Let's end this section with Nadia's story.

NADIA KADHIM

CO-FOUNDER, NAQ

FINDING THE ENERGY

Nadia is an Iraqi-Surinamese-Dutch human rights lawyer who has founded a cyber security startup. She has a powerful story and experience to match, but when I met her all of this was wrapped in a polite and understated voice. The combination of her high tone of voice and sweet smile opened the door for people to assess her as the girl who is trying hard but doesn't have what the world needs. She had a few gremlins we needed to overcome. So I asked Nadia to tell me the story of how she became co-founder of Naq. I didn't want her to give me a pitch, but just to tell it to me as a genuinely interested and captive audience – as if I had paid £1,000 for my seat to hear her speak, because I really wanted to hear what she had to say.

Within 30 seconds of her story, when I discovered that she used to be a human rights lawyer, I wanted to know how Nadia had gone from human rights lawyer to co-founder of a cyber security startup. Often, we feel the story of how we got to where we are is not valid – an accusation that our gremlins just love to throw at us.

After hearing her story, I then asked Nadia to start again, but to speak 10% faster and to use her tone of voice to highlight one word in each sentence that really mattered to her. This brought energy to her presentation and killed the 'sweet voice' I had encountered at the start. It's very common for people to speak slowly when presenting because they have been told to slow down in the past. This is so unhelpful. Slowing down is not the answer. The answer is to speak in short, sharp sentences and to pause after each sentence.

This is what Nadia had to say about her experiences with me as a coach:

> 'I was so amazed to learn that a few minor changes, such as leaning in on certain words or even talking just 10% faster, could make such a difference. I find myself thinking about Stew's wise words in every single meeting, and every single pitch I do is better because Stew is in my head. I really feel like I am becoming a storyteller. I stopped using overly-long sentences, filled with jargon, even though that goes against my nature as a lawyer. I'm becoming more creative and suddenly find myself telling visual stories, something I was always envious of in other people.'

Here are three practical actions you can take from Nadia's story:

- Find someone you feel safe and comfortable with, and simply tell the story of how you got to where you are today, in about five minutes. Imagine that you are having a cosy chat by the fire. There's no pressure. People want to hear. Force yourself to use visual imagery.
- Re-present, but now try to do it in two and a half minutes and speak 10% faster than normal, using short, sharp sentences. Don't forget to breathe at the end of each sentence!
- Deliberately over-pronounce one word in each sentence that you want people to hear.

Recording yourself is the best way of noticing the difference, and you can easily do this on your laptop or desktop. Here is a link to my online video walkie-talkie tool to help you. I have set it up so that when you hit the record button it is a private video channel. You won't get feedback from me, but just space to practise and record. Don't worry, I won't watch it!

RECORD YOURSELF
AMPLIFY.ME.UK/MIRROR

ACT II

LEAPING OFF THE CLIFF

SCENE 1

REWRITING THE SCRIPT

Thanks to your gremlins, you have formed some bad storytelling habits and the only way to break a bad storytelling habit is to create a new one. Squeezing tight, pushing a bit harder, and hoping that it will all magically change will not work.

You have to do something different.

At the end of Act I, we saw how Nadia dealt with her gremlins in a very practical way. She recognised them, chose to behave differently, and because of that choice she now tells stories and not bulleted PowerPoints! I coached her into that and gave her the techniques to do it.

Now it's your turn.

'I AM'

Let's return to your three accusations. Whatever negative accusation your gremlin has confronted you with, you are going to turn it on its head and flip it into a positive statement. Here's what I did with mine:

- *Accusation 1: 'Calm down – you're over the top.'*
- **Statement 1:** 'I have a lot of energy and I use it to bring people alive.'

- *Accusation 2: 'Why do you think you're important? That is so arrogant.'*
- **Statement 2:** 'I know that what I do transforms lives. So I will do it relentlessly.'

- *Accusation 3: 'What you do doesn't change the world, so why bother?'*
- **Statement 3:** 'I unlock people to use their own voice powerfully, and that is enough.'

I have not defended myself against Ken – I have gone over and above him to speak truth to myself. And that is powerful. So write down your accusations again and turn them into your own statements below. Don't worry if it takes a bit of time to do this, but please don't move on until you have written them down.

Accusation 1:

....

Statement 1:

....

....

Accusation 2:

....

Statement 2:

....

....

Accusation 3:

....

Statement 3:

....

....

You have your 'I am' statements. Now it's time to read them out loud. Right now.

You probably hurried through that first reading and spoke in little more than a whisper. But that is no way to defeat a gremlin. You have to speak louder. Try it again. It will feel weird – just go with it.

Now read them out again. This time, lift your head up high and speak a little louder still.

Gremlins are like ticks that need to be pulled out. Ticks are horrible parasites that can latch onto our bodies, bury their heads into our skin and refuse to let go. The only way to get them out is to grab them by their heads and pull them out. It is painful but crucial to stop yourself from catching the diseases they carry. When you feel the pain, you know that you're hitting the right spot. So, to finally pull that gremlin out, put your statements on a Post-it Note and stick them behind your computer. Remind yourself of these statements just before you switch on your computer to attend a meeting. If you are meeting in person, take a small card with you and read them in the bathroom beforehand.

Let's remind ourselves what Nadia said, after pulling out her gremlin:

'I really feel like I am becoming a storyteller. I have stopped using overly-long sentences filled with jargon, even though that goes against my nature as a lawyer. I'm becoming more creative and suddenly find myself telling visual stories, something I was always envious of in other people.'

Nadia behaved her way into freedom from her gremlins and, in her own words, is becoming more creative. You can too! And I am going to give you every tool you need to make that happen.

Let's start with your voice.

SCENE 2

USING YOUR BODY AND YOUR VOICE

In the 1960s, Albert Mehrabian conducted a study around how we communicate with our body language, voice and words. And he came up with three statistics:

- 55%
- 38%
- 7%

When we are presenting passionately about something we care about, over half of what we communicate is through our body language (55%), over a third (38%) is tonality – how we use our voices – and just 7% comes down to the *actual words we use.*

Have you ever sent a text or email that has been completely misinterpreted?

There is a reason for that. You were only working with the 7%.

Every presentation matters and needs to have an element of passion and conviction, even the ones you don't want to give. You are on display every time. They say an actor is only as good as his or her last role. If we took that attitude towards our presentations we would work hard every time.

So what was your last presentation like?

Let's unpack your 55% a little.

When did you last think about how you sit, stand, smile, lean forwards, lean back? When did you last pause to consider your posture? In fact, in all of your education, can you remember the six-week course on how to have really good body language? I doubt it.

But don't fear: we are going to fix this with some solid coaching and the help of a few transformative exercises.

Here is one simple exercise that I have used over the past decade with my clients – in fact, I have been using it myself since my acting days, 20 years ago! Let's get you on your feet and let's get your 55% strong. This exercise works. It will change your posture. More than that, it could change your life...

EXERCISE: THE STRING

WATCH VIDEO
AMPLIFY.ME.UK/STRING

1. Plant your feet on the floor so they are shoulder-width apart. Not like a cowboy and not like you are standing to attention. Allow your arms to rest by your side. If you want to keep hold of the book, keep it in one hand.
2. You are going to pretend you are a puppet on a string. How? Use one of your hands to pull a piece of imaginary string out of the top of your head. Pull it nice and tight. As you pull it tight it pulls you tight. In fact, it pulls you right up onto your tiptoes.
3. Now let the hand that pulled you up onto your tiptoes go back down to rest at the side of your body. Staying on your tiptoes, breathe in through your nose and out through your mouth.
4. Now slowly lower back down to the count of three.
5. When your heels are back on the floor, relax your shoulders. Your neck and stomach will be stretched and this is good! Breathe out, then breathe in. Feel your feet on the floor.
6. Practice makes permanent so do it again, this time counting to five as you slowly lower yourself down onto the floor.

If you do this exercise three times a week your body will start to remember – it's something called 'proprioception'. It will respond beautifully when you are in meetings and you will find that good posture becomes embedded. In turn, you will become more memorable. And who doesn't want that?

This is a practice that you can do quickly, before any presentation. If you are sitting down when you present, this exercise will keep you from collapsing your stomach and slouching. Keeping your feet planted on the floor, shoulder width apart, will instantly make you sit a little straighter. Try it now as you are sitting and reading this. You will be surprised at how powerful it is.

You are now stretched. You are standing nice and tall, and you are showing 55% as it should be shown. There is little-to-no slouching.

But you can't turn up to a meeting, stand (or sit) tall and then say nothing! You have to speak. And to speak, you have to breathe...

BREATHING

When children breathe in, they push their bellies out. We were all born breathing right and then, pretty much around the time we became teenagers (around the time we became aware of our bodies and started to feel self-conscious) we started doing it wrong.

Whether you ran into your adolescent years as a popular and confident teenager, or reluctantly crawled your way through them, the moment puberty hits is when we all started slouching. And when we started slouching we stopped connecting with our breathing, which connects to our voices, and our confidence took a big hit. Instead of breathing in confidently and letting our stomachs fill out, we held our stomachs in – because we couldn't possibly show an ounce of fat.

When you breathe in, in front of the mirror, do you let your stomach fill out and delight in how your belly looks, or do you try and hold it in?

What would it look like to return to our childlike ability to breathe in well? If you do any sport or singing you will have learnt to breathe in properly. But sport and singing are both activities that you *do*. Speaking is not just what you do but *who you are*. It is how you reveal yourself. The voice is deeply personal. It is not an activity. It requires you to fully expose who you are.

And that begins with breathing right, or breathing wrong.

EXERCISE: BREATHING

WATCH VIDEO
AMPLIFY.ME.UK/BREATHING

1. Plant your feet on the floor, making sure they are shoulder-width apart and pointing forwards. Imagine they are on skis if it helps.
2. Do the String exercise to realign your posture. Remember, you are pulling your head and body up as if you are a puppet.
3. Now hold your breath for a fraction of a second and then breathe out for five seconds, allowing all of the air to leave you.
4. When you have finished breathing out, breathe out a bit more. You will feel like a deflated balloon!
5. Close your mouth and allow your breath to come in through your nostrils. Your stomach will fill up like a balloon. You will feel like you look pregnant or bloated, but don't stop or try to hold it in. This is how sports professionals and singers breathe.
6. Breathe out again through your mouth to the count of five. Now that you can feel this new sensation of supported breathing, let's pay more attention to it. When you breathe out, imagine that somebody is pulling a sewing needle through your stomach and out behind you (I know it sounds weird, but I learnt this in drama school and it really works). If it helps, mime that sewing needle. I do this every time and it never lets me down.

7. As you breathe back in, allow that sewing needle to pull your stomach forward.
8. Do this for one minute.

Great stuff. You have unlocked your diaphragm and are ready to access your voice!

VOICE

Now that you can stand and breathe, let's get your voice connected. This is the bit that requires you to be exposed and to feel vulnerable. Vulnerable is good – this is how you truly learn to unlock your voice. Remember that what is at stake here is 38% of what you're going to communicate to your audience. Just over a third of what people will get from your presentations is tonality – how you say the words.

This matters. A lot.

EXERCISE: VOICE

WATCH VIDEO
AMPLIFY.ME.UK/VOICE

1. Plant your feet on the floor once more, making sure they are shoulder-width apart and pointing forwards.

2. Do the String one more time to realign your posture. Then take a quick breath out to expel any air. Now breathe in for five, remembering that you are sewing a needle through your stomach.
3. Now, instead of breathing out, you are going to keep your mouth closed and you are going to hum – into your lips.
4. Breathe in again, allowing that sewing needle to pull your stomach forwards. As you go to hum again, send it to a fixed point on the other side of the room, allowing your lips to tingle as you do so. If you feel the tingle in your nose you are doing a great job!
5. Breathe in again and hum again. This time, imagine that you are humming through the wall. As this is the third time, you may notice that you are starting to get tense. Avoid this by relaxing your shoulders and your mouth. Don't push. We all have naturally loud voices that have been hibernating in our diaphragms, our stomachs. All you are doing is letting it out. As you do so, my goal for you is to move the sound to the front of your mouth, not trapped in the back. If it helps, imagine that a bumble bee is buzzing around the front of your mouth...
6. Take a breath and do it one more time. This time relax more into it, and halfway through the hum open the mouth. As you open your mouth, you are going to say your name: 'MMMMY name is X.' Say it loud and say it proud. That is 100%

communication delivered well! Being able to say our own names well is essential to how we communicate who we are and how others connect with us. So this is not just a slightly bizarre exercise, this is you learning how to announce your presence.

Well done! In these few pages you have already started to defeat your gremlin, and learnt how to stand tall, breathe and use your voice. Let's meet another storytelling hero who spent two days with me in the middle of Spain, learning to do the same.

FLORENCE BRODERICK

CMO, CARTO

DEVELOPING SOFT SKILLS

Flo is not easy to impress. As soon as you meet her you can see intelligence oozing out of her – both emotional and intellectual – which means she can spot a fake a mile off. So when Flo and a group of graduates from Teléfonica were thrown into a three-day coaching workshop in a hotel outside Madrid (vaguely resembling the hotel from *The Shining*), I knew my work was cut out for me. I had to convince her, within the first minute, that I was worth investing her emotional energies in. I had to show her the communication level she was at and where I wanted to take her.

Flo came with a strong presentation style, but her strength was in danger of being wrongly perceived as dismissive and unreachable. I wanted Flo to be able to reveal her flair, her passion for work and excellence, and her care for others, all within 30 seconds of meeting someone. That meant teaching soft skills, coaching her to get to the story as soon as possible, and releasing the joyful and joy-filled voice that I knew was lurking underneath. So what did I do with Flo? I started with posture, breathing and voice exercises – the ones you have just done. This is what Flo had to say after our time together:

'Unsure of what to expect from such a workshop, I soon realised the immense value of what Amplify is doing. Stewart's energy and enthusiasm rubbed off on everyone taking part in the sessions. His feedback on my personal presentation style will be extremely valuable to me going forwards into my career. I learnt a lot about soft skills, presenting, body language, voice and attitude, and I can honestly say that I now think about all of these factors very differently since the course.'

Where is Flo today? At the time of writing, Flo has just been promoted to CMO of CARTO, a fast growing scale-up based in Spain. I have no doubt her soft skills and presentation style played a pivotal role in revealing her character and expertise to CARTO and prompted them to promote her to a role where she will have a really positive influence on many, many people.

What can you take from Flo's story?

- Do the posture, breathing and voice exercises three times a week for a month to embed them into your body.
- Use your body, breath and voice as deliberately as possible for the first 30 seconds of any meeting you have. It will set the tone for what follows.
- Over-pronounce your words and smile. It will release your voice to sound warm. These two very small changes can make the biggest difference.

SCENE 3

PICTURE, HEADLINE, DETAIL

You have crossed over the threshold of adventure into becoming a storytelling hero. You are standing tall. You are starting to attack your gremlins. As your wise mentor, who has travelled these paths before you, it is my job to guide you through this treacherous land. There are a few more battles we need to win before you will slay the final dragon of fear and become a storytelling hero. So let's pick up some weapons and defeat a few more bad habits.

We'll start with the crap elves.

Back in my acting days, in 2000, we were invited to give creative input into a show we were about to tour. We were given the opportunity to share our ideas, but we had to be warned about the crap elves. This is how they work. You have a great idea inside your head. It sits inside your brain, percolating. But when you go to sleep, the crap elves come out and steal it. So when you speak it out loud and it all sounds wrong and muddled and not as brilliant as you remember, it's not your fault, it's because of the crap elves! When one of us expressed such a creative-turned-crap idea, our team of actors would give that person a knowing look, and bat their arms as if they were trying to put out a fire.

They were beating away the crap elves.

I'll be honest, it happened to me more than anyone else. It was never my bad idea – it was the crap elves' fault! They loved hanging around me. As time wore on I came to firmly believe that the crap elves had evolved from an overnight takeover of my brain into a permanent infestation.

Gremlins are the second cousin of the crap elves and operate on the same principle, but instead of taking your ideas they take over your stories and make you sound really bad at presenting. Just because you have named your gremlin and brought it into the light doesn't mean it will give up easily. In fact, it is often at this point that they will increase their attacks in an attempt to overwhelm you. To combat this fresh onslaught, I need to give you three very important letters.

It's all about the P, the H and the D. A PhD in storytelling.

I read *Made To Stick* from Chip and Dan Heath a few years ago and the lessons I have taken from that book have proven invaluable to my clients. For convenience, I have turned my takeaways into a handy three-letter acronym which stands for:

- Picture
- Headline
- Detail

You don't need to spend seven years doing research and writing essays to get this PHD. You just need to do these exercises and put them into practice!

PICTURE

Years ago, I was coaching a German banker who needed to grab his audience's attention. It was a tough crowd – hard-nosed, passionate sales people who liked doing things their way. But they needed to make some changes. The CEO got up to speak to them at 9.00am in their main conference room. Through the floor-to-ceiling windows, you could see their flashy cars lined up outside, including the orange Porsche belonging to the CFO. This is how he began: 'Okay guys, so when it comes to sales, at the moment it's a little bit like we are driving around the back streets of Hamburg in a Porsche. We need to get out onto the Autobahn and go full throttle.'

Our brains process two-thirds of all the information they receive in picture. So: picture right now driving into the Spanish countryside. You turn off the main highway and drive up a dirt road. As you pass the gnarled olive trees on your left you come to a village and see a group of old, topless Spanish men sitting in the darkened door of the local tabac staring at you as you drive past. You go slow to avoid the women dressed in black and walking with hunched shoulders. And just as the track seems to get bumpier and bumpier – and you wonder if your tiny hire car can take it any more – you swing to the right down a hill and find that you are at the top of most astonishing ravine in the Sierra de Castril Nature Reserve. You park by the small private outdoor pool and notice the eagles soaring overhead. You can feel the strong heat of the mountain wind. You turn around and see – built right into the impenetrable cliff wall – two strong oak doors. You have found your cave house!

Were you there? Could you feel the staring eyes of the Spanish men in the tabac? Or the mountain wind, or the surprise of the cave house? That was my honeymoon in 2007, and I remember that drive very, very well! And now you do. Because that is the power of picture.

Allow me to drag you back to the sales meeting in Hamburg. All these men understood fast cars, so the metaphor my client used hit home – a Porsche is made for speed, just like our sales team is made for speed, so why are we on the back streets of Hamburg and not on the Autobahn, unleashing our true sales power? He spent 30 seconds talking about fast cars, but that was all he needed to get their brains on board.

SYSTEM 1, SYSTEM 2

Daniel Kahneman, the behavioural economics expert that I referred to in Act I, says that our brain has got two systems.[5] System 1 knows that if a tiger comes into your room you need to get out. It has an instinctive reaction. It also knows that 2+2=4 because it has learnt it. What was once new information is now intuitive. It is fast. But your System 2 is the system that makes something new become intuitive. It chews information slowly, at a jogging pace. It will happily follow a story or an idea, but only at a slow pace. If you give it too much information it will get overwhelmed and shut down. Your pupils will literally dilate.

Whether you use a metaphor, like my friend used with fast cars, or you deliberately use picture in your story, it will make a huge difference to your audience's brains. Their System 2 will thank you for it! Their pupils won't dilate. They will be able to breathe and focus, and follow what you are saying.

Why not try some metaphors now? What does your job feel like at the moment? Including contrast will help massively. If you are immediately panicking and thinking 'What? I can't do this!' here are some starters to prompt you:

'It feels like trying to push water uphill...with a rake.'

'It feels like trying to run like Usain Bolt in the 100 metres with a weight tied around my ankle.'

'It feels like having a glass of water in a hot desert.'

'It feels like I've gone from watching on a black-and-white TV to full-on HD/virtual reality.'

'It feels like going from dial-up to broadband (for anyone who remembers that!)'

'It feels like I've been riding with stabilisers and now they are off – which is terrifying but also freeing...'

It feels like...

....

....

It feels like...

....

....

It feels like...

....

....

HEADLINE

A headline, by nature, is a short sentence. Daniel Kahneman says that when we speak in long, convoluted sentences, our audiences actually become suspicious. They think we are not telling the truth. But when we speak in short, simple sentences we appear more trustworthy.

Journalists know they need to use a headline that grabs people's attention. If they don't reveal the really juicy information until halfway down the page, they are burying the lead. This is just as true with presentations.

Don't bury the lead. Make the headline short.

When I coach people, I stop them as soon as I get bored. Sometimes, if I'm feeling dramatic, I will literally walk off screen to make the point, or pretend to bang my head against a wall. Almost every time I do this and ask them for the headline, I get the same response: 'I was getting to that bit.' If you go to a theatre show and start to walk out because it's boring, can you imagine the director coming onto stage, stopping you and saying, 'Hey! Sit back down, I'm just getting to the best bit'? Of course not.

'That bit' is the headline you need at the beginning of the presentation.

'That bit' is what needs to come first.

Often, people's last sentence needs to be their first.

LINE FIVE TO LINE ONE

Since lockdown began I have played 'Line Five to Line One' almost every day. It is really simple – take your last line and put it first. Don't bury the lead, let your headline out. If it feels awkward to say it, it is probably right. The audience won't feel awkward. They don't know the gremlins you're battling and the sweat that is trickling down your back, but they will know when a headline has landed well. They will thank you by listening to you.

Why not do this with a simple example. Tell the story of what you did last weekend, but write it down in chronological order – in the order the events happened.

Here is my real life example:

1. We got a puppy in November and have been getting up early every morning.
2. On Christmas morning we chose to ignore Sully's barks and have a lie in.
3. We came downstairs to open up our stockings but were met with trampled dog poo all over the kitchen floor.
4. Sully's thoughtful gift definitely made for a different Christmas morning.
5. We are never going to ignore our dog barking at 6.00am again.

Now I am going to move line five to line one.

5. We are never going to ignore our dog barking at 6.00am again.
1. We got a puppy in November and have been getting up early every morning.
2. On Christmas morning we chose to ignore Sully's barks and have a lie in.
3. We came downstairs to open up our stockings but were met with trampled dog poo all over the kitchen floor.
4. Sully's thoughtful gift definitely made for a different Christmas morning.

Can you see the difference? It creates a sense of what Donald Miller calls a 'story gap'.[6] Why am I never going to ignore my dog barking at 6.00am? It sounds a bit dramatic. What happened? Then I tell the story, and there is already a sense of anticipation that draws my listeners along with me. And there is also a strong ending. All I did was move line five to line one. Our line five, 'that bit' that we think is the conclusion, is in fact the headline. It's genius!

Give it a go. Write down your five sentences in chronological order, then flip it and see what happens.

1. ....

2. ....

3. ....

4. ....

5. ....

5. ....

1. ....

2. ....

3. ....

4. ....

DETAIL

I once had a client who started his presentation like this: 'We are a global company and we need to have a global mindset to be the best player in the energy market.' There was no detail, no story. And if you have a brain like mine, just reading that opener made your brain go a bit fuzzy. It either switched off completely or was fumbling about in the dark, trying really hard to find the light switch.

After some coaching, my client confessed to me that he didn't know how to tell stories: 'I am not good at connection. I have not told stories before because *I* know them and don't think they are relevant to my audience.'

We started looking for the red thread – the piece of thread woven through him that linked his personal life with business.

This is what he re-presented:

'For me, it is really hard to call a place home. My parents are Italian, I was born in Venezuela, brought up in Portugal. My family is spread out all over the world, from Panama to Italy. I speak Spanish to my brother and Italian to my mother. Having this global family meant I had to get my own software re-programmed. I had to have a global mindset. And that's great, because I feel at home here. We need to have a global mindset because we are a global player in the energy market.'

His feedback: 'I know this creates connection with my audience.'

How did he do it? He created context and contrast.

CONTEXT

Context is the who, what, where and when. In my story, which I shared with you in Act I, I used context a lot. When talking about that assembly, I asked myself four questions:

What had happened before this moment? I had been bullied for five years, but had acted and spoken in assemblies so this was a long time coming.

Where was I, physically, in this moment? I was in the Memorial Hall, alongside a 50-foot wooden organ.

Who else was there? 600 teenage boys in dark navy suits.

When did this happen? When I was 18 years old.

I used those questions to help me fill out the details. Those details might not feel important to the point you are trying to make, but they are the paints and the brushstrokes with which you bring colour to your canvas. They are picture, and remember that your brain is wired to process two thirds of information in picture. Maybe you can already hear your gremlin whispering in your ear: 'This is a stupid exercise. It makes no difference.' Choose not to listen to it. Instead, let's do an experiment. Use the following questions to help you create context for what happened to you yesterday.

What happened in the lead up to yesterday?

....

....

....

Where were you yesterday (describe the geography of the place)?

....

....

....

Who else was there (physically or digitally)?

....

....

....

Walk us through your day, from morning, noon and night. What did you do?

....

....

....

You now have detail to play with. You have the raw material. So let's turn this into a masterpiece!

CONTRAST

Back in November 2021, in the opening of COP26, Txai Suruí had two and a half minutes to make an impact on 100 world leaders. She didn't go for abstracts or facts, she went for contrast. She started with this: 'My father told me that we must listen to the stars, the wind, the animals and the trees. Today the climate is warming, the animals are disappearing, the rivers are dying. The earth is speaking.' It was raw and unforgettable. And powerful. Because she used contrast.

Contrast is very powerful. It does something to our souls. So let's find the contrast in your 'what happened yesterday' story. By focusing on contrast you are learning new habits that will speak louder than the lies of your gremlin.

Here are a few of the contrasts in my story:

- The contrast of asking Mr Stubbs to say nothing and him standing me up in front of my entire class.
- The contrast of expecting boos when I spoke in the assembly with the reality of thunderous applause.
- The contrast in Mia's ability to present, going from shy to confident.
- The contrast between coaching teenagers and CEOs.

Take a look at your 'what I did yesterday' story and find one contrast. Just one. We only ever need one. Then write it down. And if you find more – keep writing. Scribble them down!

THE GRADUATION

You may not have realised it but I guarantee that in your 'what happened yesterday' story you will have included elements of P, H and D. You need freedom to play with your story using PHD, and that is what you got. Now go and find someone and tell them your story, using Picture, Headline and Detail. Enjoy describing the context and playing with contrast, and see how you light them up! Don't forget to stand tall, do the String, breathe and hum before you start. To send you on your way, I want to introduce you to a very special woman who also needed to learn how to play with her story. Meet Felicia!

FELICIA JACKSON

FOUNDER, CPR WRAP

GETTING PLAYFUL

Felicia nearly lost her child through a choking accident. After that, she had a vivid dream about creating something that she could put into the hands of other parents, carers, teachers

– everyone – to stop that ever happening to someone else. That is a powerful story. And the first thing I do when I coach people is to get them to tell me their story. Don't pitch it or try to impress me, just tell me the story. You can see people relax, turn off their 'serious presenting voice' and get real. These stories always carry a heart and soul. That was my experience with Felicia. It was a stunning story with huge stakes. Felicia was preparing to pitch to Steve Case, founder of AOL and pretty much the man who made the internet legal. This pitch was going to be the game changer for her.

High, high stakes.

And in the stifling heat of Chattanooga, US, just before Felicia was due to present, everything began to fall apart. She had stumbled through the dress rehearsal but her voice was betraying a complete lack of confidence in herself, and the story didn't sound genuine. Yet the reality was that CPR Wrap was saving lives and she knew it. She had given up everything to pursue this dream because she knew how much it mattered.

I had to get her to centre herself, so we did some breathing exercises – the one I got you to do earlier. I then asked her to visualise being on stage and to go through the entire pitch in her head. This can take a few minutes but if your brain can see you doing it, it will remember this when you are presenting for real.

As she was walking through her pitch, I then asked Felicia to underline certain words. This was not the time to bring in anything new, but just to encourage the very best out of what was already there. Because we share the same faith, I prayed for her. I then sent her off on her own – a pitch walk, I call it – to allow the story to become part of her body. As we have said, 55% of what we present is body language, 38% is tonality – it is never just the words. And as she was walking, I saw her start to embody it. I saw her start to play with the pitch and to feel it flow through her.

This is what Felicia says about the experience:

'I had pitched in front of many crowds, small and large, but pitching in front of Steve Case on a national platform – the exposure alone was monumental for my small startup.

'We had one full day to practise with Stewart, and a few hours before our actual pitch to work on tone and voice projection. It was my turn to get on the stage to practise but as I looked out into the pavilion something happened to me that I still can't explain. As I started to speak the first sentence of my pitch I heard the deafening pounding of my heart. My mouth was dry and my words wouldn't leave my lips. I started to panic! I couldn't just push through the fear like I always did so I bolted towards the door, with Stewart right behind me. He took my hand and we both sat on a bench outside of the pavilion, and that's when my emotions exploded and I started to cry.

> 'At that point, I felt defeated and embarrassed, and knew I could not go on stage in front of a packed venue. I don't know what Stewart said, but I know he gave me a shoulder to cry on. I went on stage that night to a packed, standing-room-only pavilion and pitched my heart out! I made eye contact, my voice was strong and I told my story in a way that only I could. Stewart not only worked on polishing my pitch and presentation but he also worked on me building my inner confidence... He helped me believe in myself and, for that, I am forever grateful.'
>
> Felicia's confidence, the power, the playfulness and the joy – it was infectious! CPR Wrap has gone from strength to strength. At the time of writing, they have delivered 12,000 life-saving kits and Felicia has been named one of the Forbes Next 1000. It feels like this is just the beginning for her! Every time I see her face on LinkedIn I don't just see a woman brimming with confidence, I see a storytelling hero who battled hard and deep to bring this story and this incredible life-saving device to the world.

What can you learn from Felicia? Here are three exercises to encourage you to play with your presentations.

- Focus yourself by sitting down and planting your feet firmly on the floor, shoulder-width apart. Breathe in for five seconds, hold it, then breathe out.

- Visualise yourself on the stage – whether it's an auditorium stage, a theatre, a pub, or a computer screen. Visualise delivering the entire pitch from beginning to end. Allow a few minutes to do this. Go all the way to the end of your presentation. It will feel weird but it works! As you deliver the pitch, imagine underlining certain words and phrases that stick out to you.
- Now take your pitch out for a walk. Put some headphones in, pretend you are on the phone and speak it out. Start with a Headline, enjoy painting the Picture and giving the Detail. Have fun with it. Practise putting the emphasis on the words that you want to stand out. Walking will make all of this easier to do. Walk fast as you pitch. Deliver your presentation two or three times until you really start to feel the flow instinctively, like Felicia did. Feeling the flow gives you the freedom to play with your story, and when you play you are unforgettable.

ACT III

APPROACHING THE DRAGON'S LAIR

SCENE 1

LISTEN OUT

You are deep into your journey now. You have your new PHD storytelling tools in your arsenal, you are awake to the gremlins all around you, you are standing tall and breathing well. You have started to tell mini stories, and have learnt from fellow travellers that you have met along the way, taking on their practical tools to overcome fear and present like a storytelling hero.

Before I unleash you to tell your own story, I want to give you a storytelling tool that transformed me back in 2016 – it transformed my marriage, my parenting and my business. It literally changed my life, and I use it every day in every story I tell. It could do the same for you.

THE SUPERPOWER OF LISTENING

Before I learnt to listen in order to understand, I used to listen in order to reply. I couldn't wait for the person on the other side of the conversation to finish before I jumped in! What I had to say was clearly more important than what they had to say, or even if it wasn't more important, I knew what the other person was going to say and they were taking a *long* time to say it. I would poke and probe until I got the answer out of them. Then my friend Richard Garnett, founder of GBS Comms, invited me to a listening workshop he was delivering. It was brilliant.

And that was when I discovered it. I was a prober. I was so keen to get to know people that I would prod and poke until I got the information out of them. I went up to Richard at the end and declared, 'I'm a prober!' Graciously, he said, 'Stew, you are a work in progress.'

I went home that night and practised what I had learnt on my wife, Liz. I asked her about her day and then tried very hard to listen to understand. Afterwards, she said, 'What have you done?'

I said, 'What do you mean?'

'Well the kids aren't screaming and I feel completely listened to.'

I am going to tell you right now what I did, so that you can do the same with every person you speak to. If you can listen really well, then you have a right to share your story and to know which bit of it to share. And that makes for a very powerful storyteller. What I say here is inspired by Steven Covey's *Seven Habits of Highly Effective People* – habit five of which is 'Seek first to understand'. Please, please read it. It is rare and beautiful wisdom. But for now, let me introduce you to APE.

AIR

I love connecting, so when I feel excited I want to finish Liz's sentence for her. But that's not giving air. That's taking air. Giving air to someone is giving them an invitation to speak and allowing them time to do it. I love talking, so interrupting is a natural hazard I have to learn to avoid. I avoided this in my conversation with Liz by giving her air. I asked how her day was and let her speak. I didn't interrupt. Always invite your audience to share something.

PLAYBACK

As Liz talked, my next challenge was just to *playback*. She started talking about the stress of dropping the kids off at school, getting on the London Underground, the busyness, the heat, the exhaustion of doing it all and then doing it again at the end of the day. Instead of me interrupting and saying, 'I know, I know, it's a nightmare! When I did it yesterday – oh my gosh, the body odour was awful,' I held my tongue a bit longer than I normally would.

Liz kept talking.

Instead of probing and asking, 'How long was the journey back? What station did you get off at?' I kept quiet and demonstrated with my body language that I cared – because I did! I started to feel her pain and frustration. I wanted to keep her talking so I used the B word: 'because'. It wasn't a direct question. It encouraged her to keep talking without me taking things off on my own track. Then I did something that most of my clients hate doing.

I played it back: the whole school-drop-off-London-Underground-repeat-sweaty-people journey.

Playback is not commenting.

Playback is not interpreting.

Playback is also not repeating like a parrot.

I used different language but told the same story through her eyes. I said, 'So you dropped the kids off, rushed to the train and the Underground, were surrounded by sweaty people and felt exhausted before your day had even begun. You only had three hours before doing it all over again, and you had to check your emails on the way back, which is the last thing you wanted to do because you were trying to put down the day before picking up the kids.'

Then I showed empathy.

EMPATHY

As Steven Covey describes it, empathy is seeing the world through the eyes of the person who is speaking, through their lens. Walking the world in their shoes. So my response to Liz was, 'That just sounds exhausting.' Then I did something equally revolutionary.

I said nothing.

I let her lead me.

When I was silent, Liz used the B word on herself. She said, 'It was exhausting, because I just feel like I am getting nothing done and I hate turning up to the kids and not really being present.'

When you get a 'because' you know the person in front of you is peeling off the layers and revealing what they are feeling. At that moment, I had to choose to resist asking a question (remember, I am a prober so it is my natural, untaught state), or offer a solution. I had to choose to keep peeling the onion, to keep playing back. It felt unnatural and a bit forced, but it really helped Liz talk.

I played back to Liz what she said: 'So you are feeling like you can't really get anything done and you aren't present for the kids as a mum.' We then had a profound conversation about her struggles with being both a mum and the leader of a charity. We talked deep and long and that is what led her to say, 'I feel completely listened to.'

This book is about storytelling, and as I am guiding you through various enemies it would have been an oversight not to include the enemy of bad listening. Bad listening is one of the things that will stop you from being a great storyteller. Because you won't be able to sense what your audience needs. Because if you are not listening to your audience when they speak, you are probably not listening to yourself when you speak. If you can listen well, you can know which story to tell, or which bit. That is true connection.

The next time you ask someone you love about their day, take time to play back and get them to use the B word. It will surprise you! Then apply it to business and you will actually hear what the other person is thinking. And when you know what they need, you can then tell them the right story. It can transform your business (but more on that in Act V).

By the end of this book, you will be able to listen profoundly and tell your story brilliantly – the right story at the right time to move your audience to action. But first, let's tame the beast of adrenaline and learn how to use it to our advantage.

SCENE 2

CHANNELLING YOUR ADRENALINE

Back in 2000, I spent 15 months on tour as an actor. We performed in schools, prisons, church halls, old people's homes, leisure centres – pretty much anywhere other than an actual theatre! We performed our show over 1,000 times, to many different audiences. Old people who couldn't hear. Young people who didn't care. Prisoners who weren't afraid to let you know if they liked you or not. There was always something at stake.

Every time, just before I went out onto the 'stage' in front of me, my teeth would go numb. Has that ever happened to you? It is the weirdest sensation. And my stomach would start to flip. It was adrenaline kicking in and firing through my system. Apparently, the amount of adrenaline an actor feels just before they go on stage is the equivalent to having a heart attack! I would sometimes ask myself, 'Why am I doing this to my body?' But then I would step on stage and channel that adrenaline into my performance. It was amazing. There is nothing quite like that experience. But I also got paid to go through that daily journey. It was my job.

It's not your job. You might be an accounts manager, an administrative executive, or a charity leader. You don't get paid to experience this. Yet you almost certainly will experience it every time you present. Adrenaline is great in so many ways. It senses threat and protects you, it helps you work towards deadlines and tells you to flee from burning buildings. But it doesn't know the difference between physical and emotional threat. When you are presenting, it thinks you are under attack and goes into defense mode. It shuts your body and voice down. It will cause you to forget what you wanted to say or turn your words into nonsense. It will make you inhibited and a shadow of yourself. Unless you learn to control it. Or tame it. Over the years I have seen adrenaline controlled and channelled to create stunning moments of freedom in speaking. Here are three steps that will help you do just that.

1. LOOK THE STALLION IN THE EYE

Adrenaline is like a stallion, that powerful black horse that thunders through the valley and is a wonder to behold. Untamed, it is wild and you can't go near it. But when tamed by a skilful rider, it can do incredible things. The untamed stallion rides all over your speech patterns, the words you use, the uncertain pauses, the unfinished sentences. But you can't tame something that you can't see. You have to shine a light on it.

Write down your top five bad habits when it comes to presenting.

You might mumble.

Or forget to breathe.

Your sentences might be too long and trail off at the end…

You might not look at the audience.

Whatever you do, write down your top five.

1.
....

....

2.
....

....

3.
....

....

4.

....

....

5.

....

....

2. MAKE RIDICULOUS RULES

The great thing about a habit is that it is possible to change! The way we are going to change these bad habits into good habits is to first turn each one into a ridiculous rule. Let's imagine that you have actually written yourself a set of rules, ridiculous rules, that you have told yourself you have to follow every time you do a presentation. So, if you mumble, one of your rules is this:

'I must always mumble.'

No-one actually does this intentionally, but we do it subconsciously, don't we? Our bad habits are really just a series of rules we follow that have become ingrained in how we speak. As you write this rule, use language that is dramatic. Here is a dramatic version of the mumble rule:

'I must, at all times, mumble, never speak clearly, and make sure I never, *ever* end my sentences.'

If your next bad habit is 'No structure' then you could write down:

'It is my aim to totally confuse my audience by not ever letting them know where I am going. I must *never* have any clear structure to my presentations.'

You get the idea. So let's do it! Take those five bad habits, turn them into ridiculous rules and write them down here.

1. ....

....

2. ....

....

3. ....

....

4. ....

....

5.
....

....

Now you have done that, read them out loud as dramatically as possible. Record it on your phone and send it over to me at Amplify (stewart@amplify.me.uk). Go on, I dare you. Let's have some fun with this. Because it is through humour that you are going to tame this stallion and unlock the storytelling hero within, to face your public-speaking dragon!

3. CREATE NEW RULES

'I WILL'

To deal with the gremlins back in Act I, we wrote down some 'I am' statements. To tame adrenaline, we need some 'I will' statements. Let's flip your five ridiculous rules into five storytelling aspirations – new habits that you are going to walk into.

Remember my first rule? 'I must, at all times, mumble, never speak clearly and make sure I never, *ever* end my sentences.' This is how I would flip it with an 'I will':

'I will speak clearly, in short, sharp sentences.'

It is a concise aspirational statement. It is one I can remember, keep myself accountable to, and one that I can put on a Post-it Note behind my computer. Let's do the same with yours. Take your five ridiculous rules and turn them into five 'I wills'.

1. ....

....

2. ....

....

3. ....

....

4. ....

....

5. ....

....

If you were to focus on just one of these new rules, once a week, and if you were to put that new rule on a Post-it Note where you can see it as you present, it would transform all your presentations. So write it down and have it handy as we enter the dragon's lair. It's time to meet Freya.

FREYA WATSON

DRAGON-SLAYER

EMBRACING VULNERABILITY

Freya is a dragon-slayer, but it wasn't always that way. At the age of 15, she was so shy in school that at break time she would hide in the toilet and lift her feet up off the floor, so no-one knew she was there.

Then she went to a conference for young leaders and was blown away by this idea that leadership and vulnerability could actually work together. You didn't have to be fake, or post the right thing on the right social network – being yourself and telling your story was enough. You didn't have to be picture-perfect or popular. You had to be real.

So, step by step, she peeled herself open. She stopped hiding in the toilets and started hanging out with people. She said to her friend, 'This is not about popularity. This is about loving the person in front of me.' A year later, she decided to apply to be school captain, and to her complete shock she was voted in by her friends and teachers! The girl who had resorted to hiding in the toilet stalls was now the girl leading her school into vulnerability and honesty.

She then went on a week-long residential with the same charity that had taught her about leadership, just before she went off to university in 2021. One of the highlights of this week was learning the art of soft skills, like listening to people. At the freshers' fair, she made the deliberate choice simply to remember people's names and take time to listen. This went completely against the grain of the 'I'm going to listen to you until I meet someone else more interesting' university culture she was surrounded by.

To her surprise, people came up to her to actually thank her for listening to them. She brought her fight for leadership and her captaincy of the school onto the university campus, and started to lead there too.

When she shared this story at the charity's fundraiser, in November 2021, there was pin-drop silence. Well actually, that's not quite accurate. There was a gasp when she talked about hiding in the toilets and tears when she shared how she had not only become captain but was seeking to live with purpose in her life now. That night, the charity raised £113,000 from 80 people in the room – by far the biggest amount to date, with the smallest number of people attending![7]

The power of a story, lived out and told well, is almost immeasurable. Except that we measured it that night.

> I coached Freya to tell her story and it went from quite good to deeply compelling. What did I do? She had been asked a series of questions and to every question there was, at first, an answer that was too long. I asked her to tell me the answers to each question in one and a half minutes. Every answer had to have one story within it. Often when we present we feel we have to explain the answer first and then back it up with a story. This is a lie! It needs to be the other way round. Restricting Freya to only a minute and a half for each answer forced her to leap right in with the story. She then spoke in headlines to drive home the point she wanted to make.

You are about to embark on telling your own story. As you go about this, it will feel like you are facing a dragon breathing the fires of comparison, or lies from the gremlin. Don't be fooled. Allow Freya to journey with you as you persevere. If she did it, so can you. If she told her story with power and slayed the dragon, you can do it too.

It's time to pick up your sword.

What can you learn from Freya's story? Ask yourself three questions about three events in your life that most affected you and that (eventually) led to a positive change. Restrict yourself to answering in one and a half minutes. Record it as an audio note and play it back!

SCENE 3

APPROACHING THE DRAGON: CREATING YOUR HERO'S JOURNEY STORY

In J. R. R. Tolkein's *The Hobbit*, Bilbo travels on an epic journey to steal some treasure from a dragon. Even before he gets to the dragon's lair he has had to fight a fair few enemies. Now he has to confront the dragon itself. Being faced with a dragon is not easy. You have to have your wits about you. It will take everything you have because it threatens your very existence. It doesn't want to give you the treasure and is prepared to breathe fire on you to make sure you never get your hands it.

Up to this point, I have been preparing and equipping you with a solid storytelling toolkit. You have already won some battles – you know your gremlin, you know how to stand tall and use your voice, you have gained a PHD in storytelling, and you are learning to tame the stallion of adrenaline.

You will need all of that for what is about to come.

Your treasure is your story, told incredibly well to your audiences. Your dragon is a toxic mixture of fear and comparison, and if it breathes on you it will melt you. We can't let that happen. Just as Bilbo confronts the dragon, finds its weak spot, and eventually comes away with the treasure, we are going to do that now – through your Hero's Journey.

YOUR HERO'S JOURNEY

As we glimpsed in Act I, the Hero's Journey of Hollywood goes something like this: our potential hero/heroine has to make a decision to act – Katniss Everdeen steps up to take the place of her sister in the brutal Games, Luke Skywalker chooses to rescue Princess Leia and help the Rebel Alliance against the oppressive Empire, Frodo volunteers to take the one ring to Mordor…

At some point, each one of these heroes falls into a pit of despair and is totally lost, until they meet a wise mentor who helps them to discover the inner strength that has been a part of them all along – Haymitch shows Katniss how to hone her skills and become a warrior with a fighting chance, Yoda trains Luke to tune in to the Force within him, to resist the dark side and to embrace his destiny as a Jedi Knight, and Gandalf tells Frodo: 'You must trust yourself. Trust your own strengths.' Then, when our hero knows who they are and recognises the strength and power they carry, they take up their sword, slay the dragon, find the treasure, and emerge into a new land!

They started out ordinary, but now they are the hero.

I love the Hero's Journey because it has a clear beginning, middle and end. It is filled with picture and emotion and we all, at some point, recognise the hero's struggles.

I also love IKEA – it makes me feel like a master builder. Even when I'm on the point of rage because there's a tiny but essential bolt missing from my box, I inevitably find that it was there all along, hiding somewhere at the bottom of the bag. Here are my IKEA-style instructions for building your own Hero's Journey story. You may well think there is a bolt missing, or doubt how it's all going to come together.

Keep going. Trust the process.

Your story, told well, is the treasure in your quest. And the technique you are about to learn will help you to tell any story for any audience, anywhere.

Let's start with the question, 'How did I get to where I am today?'

I have never seen anyone talk about their life using abstract terms. People don't come into the kitchen after a hard day's work and present a PowerPoint to their loved ones! Yet when we talk about business we so often fall into that trap. We forget about our beginnings, middles and endings and we go into default 'boring' mode. Adrenaline takes over, the gremlins come out to play, and we feel worthless. But forcing yourself right now to tell your story in two and a half minutes, with the key ingredients of beginning, middle and end, will set you on course for trampling your gremlins, taming adrenaline and speaking with confidence. And that's what we are going to do.

I watched Richard Garnett do a version of this exercise where he suggested imagining your life in six bubbles, or six scenes. This is absolute genius and we are going to borrow from Richard's wisdom here. Bubble one is your beginning, bubble three your middle, and bubble six your end. In each bubble I am going to ask you to write down a phrase or series of words that describe that particular moment or scene in your life. Here are the six bubbles that I wrote down to help me create my Hero's Journey:

BUBBLE 1
Mr Stubbs stands me up

BUBBLE 2
Being shouted out of classrooms

BUBBLE 3
The Assembly in the Memorial Hall

BUBBLE 4
Coaching Mia

BUBBLE 5
Amplify's journey of coaching clients

BUBBLE 6
My motivation when I coach TODAY

It absolutely wasn't a script. It was just a series of words. They were my prompt to help me tell my story – to get me from the beginning to the middle, and through to the end. Over the page are six blank bubbles, ready and waiting for you to write a catchphrase in each. Let's add in the layer of the Hero's Journey and you might find that bubble one is just before the pit of despair. As you travel through your life you encounter allies, troubles, wise mentors, and eventually slay the dragon. And that's how you got to where you are today. If I was to place my six bubbles within the Hero's Journey it would look like this:

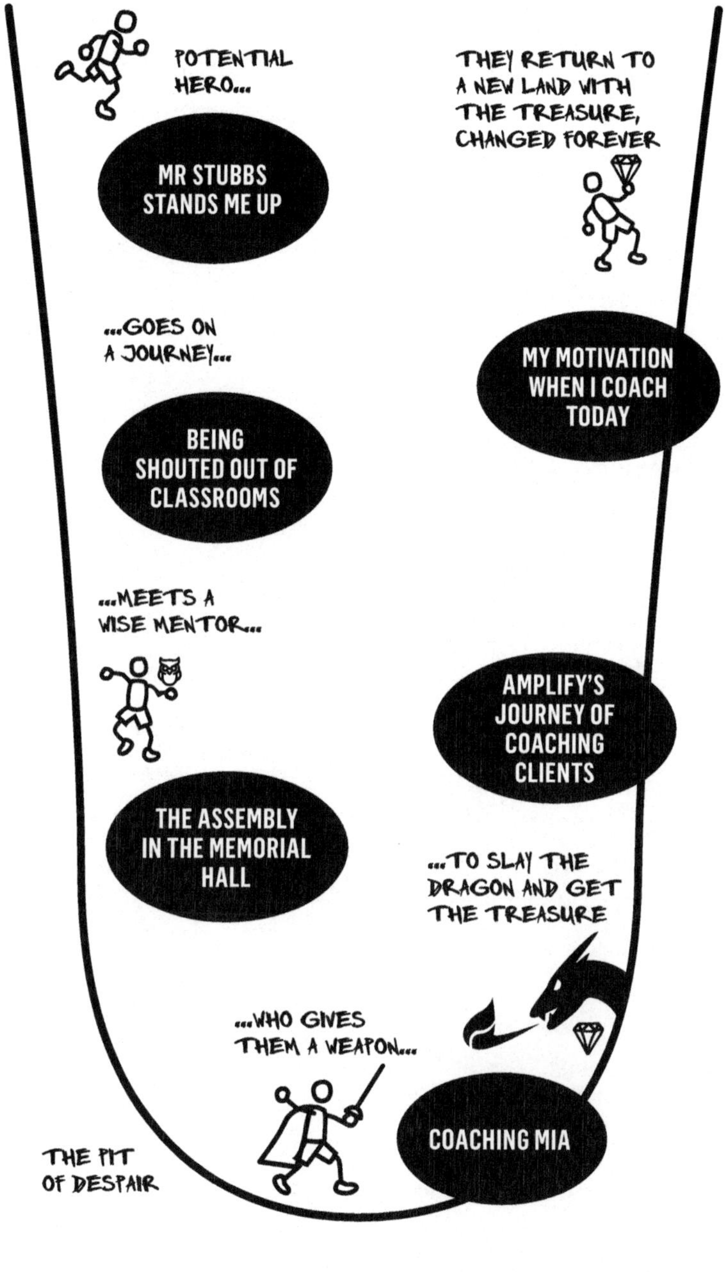
POTENTIAL HERO...
MR STUBBS STANDS ME UP
...GOES ON A JOURNEY...
BEING SHOUTED OUT OF CLASSROOMS
...MEETS A WISE MENTOR...
THE ASSEMBLY IN THE MEMORIAL HALL
...WHO GIVES THEM A WEAPON...
THE PIT OF DESPAIR
COACHING MIA
...TO SLAY THE DRAGON AND GET THE TREASURE
AMPLIFY'S JOURNEY OF COACHING CLIENTS
MY MOTIVATION WHEN I COACH TODAY
THEY RETURN TO A NEW LAND WITH THE TREASURE, CHANGED FOREVER

Now it's over to you. Let the first memory be whatever it wants to be – you might be five, you might be 15, you might find yourself at university or working on a shop floor when something happened to spark a journey.

You may be tempted to cover your story in four or five bubbles, but try to do it in six. You may want to write more words than I did – go for it! You might want to draw pictures or create a timeline. Get as creative as you want to. Just make sure that what you end up with is a two-and-a-half-minute story.

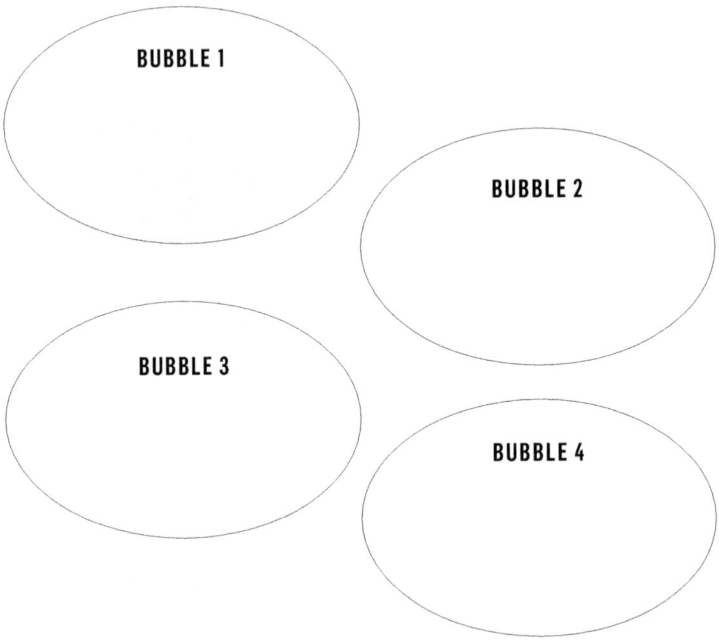

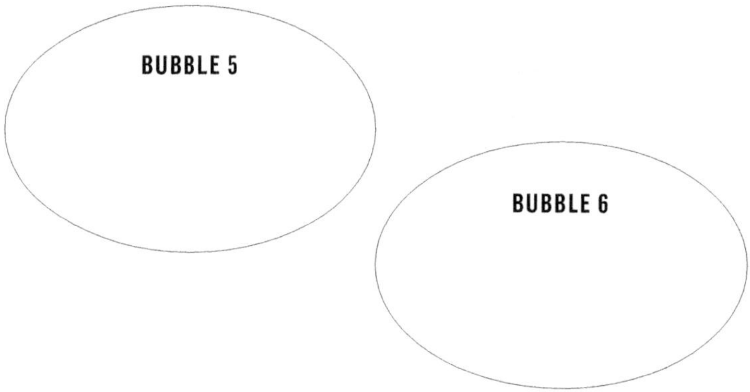

Be careful not to turn this into a script – it is only meant to be a prompt. Now it is time to speak it out. Remember that it must be no longer than two and a half minutes. If you want to practise, go to my website where you can record your video as if talking to the mirror. You won't get any feedback from me and I won't be collecting your data. If you want to delete it, you can delete it afterwards. It's just a very helpful tool for you to feel the pressure of having to tell a story when the red button is on!

RECORD YOURSELF
AMPLIFY.ME.UK/MIRROR

I can't put you into breakout rooms or send you off in pairs so I am going to ask you to do two things to make sure you speak this out:

1. Get your phone out, put it on your mantelpiece and get ready to hit record OR open up your laptop, start

a meeting with yourself on Zoom/Teams/Google Meet and hit record.

2. Once you have done it, find a friend (online or offline) and ask them to listen to your recording as a kind of 'guinea pig' audience. You can totally blame me – tell them your coach has made you do it! Remember, the voice is something that is deeply, deeply personal so only share your recording with someone you trust.

This is the moment. Go!

To help and encourage you with this, I would love you to meet Derrick. Let his story inspire you to tell yours.

DERRICK A. PARSON

FOUNDER, GRASPIE

OVERCOMING EXPECTATIONS

Derrick is a presence in any room – six feet tall (at least), larger than life – and when I met him at the Google for Startups: Black Founder Exchange in North Carolina I was deeply impressed. That was the problem. I sensed that he felt he was having to live up to something – an impressive image he projected, a confidence that was based more on swagger than on his authentic story. Over 20 minutes I gently tugged and pushed and pulled and we had the most profound conversation. It became one of my podcast recordings: a journey into vulnerability that was an honour to be part of.

He used to get really, really nervous before pitching. He would look happy and unfazed on the outside, but the reality would be a very different story. Nine times out of ten, after a pitch he couldn't even remember what he had said.

We asked 'Derrick the presenter' to step out of the room and brought in Derrick the person. That meant not standing up and pitching, but sitting down, leaning in to me and telling me, quietly, the story of the problem he was solving. A bit like those late night deep-and-meaningfuls where someone has dropped the polite exterior and is bearing their soul. It changed his language from *impressive* to *real*. He couldn't talk at me, he had to talk to me. He went from a caricature to a real person. When he delivered his final pitch, 24 hours later, he brought the energy to that intimacy and was very believable.

It was a night-and-day transformation and we got to the real problem he was trying to solve: boring staff training, and how to get people super engaged. There was a bit of singing, a lot of joy, and a real unlocking.

Here's what he had to say:

> 'Your coaching was a guiding light. It helped me to not only find my true voice but to let that be the centre of attention, and not my larger-than-life demeanour.'

What can you take from Derrick's coaching and put into your story?

- Pull up a chair in front of you.
- Have a conversation with that chair, imagining somebody is only about half a metre away from you. Tell the chair your Hero's Journey.
- Do it again, and this time talk quietly and intimately – even whisper.
- Record yourself so that you can see the transformation. You will see PHD pouring out of you.
- Re-tell your story based on the new headlines that came out of the bubbles exercise. It will have more of a storytelling, conversational flow and less of a 'talking at you' tone. If it feels exposing, you're doing it right. That is how Derrick felt and it's what made his final presentation so very powerful.

Now find that trusted human and go tell your story!

ACT IV

THE ROAD BACK

SCENE 1

BECOMING BRILLIANT AT TELLING YOUR STORY

In the movies, there is always this beautiful moment towards the end where the skies clear, the rain disappears, all evil is vanquished and the hero or heroine embarks on the road back home. The hero has slain that dragon but the film isn't over yet. They are returning to a new, promised land.

Because everything is different. For them.

And the same is true for you. To help you enjoy this road back to a new and promised land, away from the pit of despair, I am going to ask you to tell your story to as many people as possible. Because practice makes permanent.

You have been on an epic journey, and it's all been preparing you for this moment. You have named your gremlin, learnt how to make your 55% body language, 38% tonality and

7% spoken words land with your audience, you have created your own Hero's Journey, and you have recorded that journey. You have learnt how to do storytelling holistically, with the power tool of listening. You have slain the dragon because you have presented that story live to someone else. You have found that human, tamed that adrenaline, pulled out those gremlins, stood tall, and put everything you have learnt into practice by telling that person your two and a half minute story. The only way a story lives, according to J. K. Rowling, is if someone hears it. And yours is living. Now it's time for you to journey back.

Here are four ways to get your story into your bones.

1. **Take your story out for a walk with your notes.** It can help to put in headphones so that other people think you are talking to someone, and you feel less self-conscious. They don't need to know that you are presenting to yourself and to the air around you! As you talk and walk, you will feel which bits flow easily and which bits are hard.
2. **Tell your story again, with no notes.** Keep walking with it. When you find the bits that are hard to remember, rewind and try telling that hard part again. There will often be one sentence that keeps tripping you up. Either abandon it or rephrase it.
3. **For those spots where you feel you can't remember what comes next, you need a strong linking sentence.**

Phrases like, 'Five years later…', 'It took a month, but in the end it was worth it, because…', or even, 'So…' are good sentence starters. Practise them by deliberately over-pronouncing each word of that line.

4. **Increase your pace by 10%.** This will stop you from going into autopilot. Increasing pace doesn't mean saying your words at 1.5 speed. It means breathing and pausing at the end of your sentences, rather than in the middle.

ADVANCED POSTURE EXERCISES

You are reading this book not because you want to be able to tell a story to entertain your friends, but because you want to influence your peers and seniors, you really want that promotion, that contract or that funding. You want to convince or motivate people. That is the real-world power of storytelling.

You may feel that your voice is hidden in the corporate world or you may feel you are so exposed that you have nowhere safe to road-test your presentations. Remember Kumi, right back at the start of our journey together? She had a voice but couldn't find it. Once she discovered and unleashed it, it exposed her to audiences that she had only dreamt of. So, on this road back, let's apply this to the presentations we need to deliver in business. When the stakes are higher, our storytelling skill needs to be greater.

You have been using your voice and you have learnt some good presentation skills. Now let's take you to James Bond 007 level, to *Mission: Impossible* jumping-out-of-a-helicopter level.

Here is an exercise that is absolutely brilliant. I did this every day on tour, whether we were in prisons, school halls or – on the odd occasion – on the street. It took away the tension in my shoulders and helped me to breathe in deeply.

EXERCISE: THE FLOP

When I am stressed and tired, and my shoulders are particularly tense, I force myself to do this exercise because I know, despite the pain, that it will literally straighten me out. It will unleash my 55% and make me ready to engage people. Your mission, should you choose to accept it, is to do this exercise right now. And as you do it, remember that you are in good company. Michael Caine does this before every film take, and he's done pretty well out of it![8]

1. Stand with your feed wide apart and reach up with your hands to try to touch the ceiling.
2. Flop over slowly, like a puppet being cut from a string, to the count of eight. Your hands flop first, then let your arms flop gently to your sides, then your

head flops forward, bringing with it your shoulders, chest and finally your waist.

3. Breathe in and breathe out slowly five times. As you breathe try to touch your toes. If you can't, it doesn't matter. It's about stretching your back.
4. To stay relaxed and to stretch your back, allow your arms to move around from left to right like you are a monkey for a few seconds.
5. Now it's time to roll back up to standing with your arms by your side, to a slow count of eight. Roll up putting your hips in place first, then your stomach, your chest and finally, roll your chin off your chest and let your head up last.
6. Close your eyes and breathe in. Feel your feet on the floor. You are aligned and will feel how tall you actually are when you don't slouch! This is so good for making sure we are looking after our bodies.

Practise makes permanent, so do the whole thing again, but this time roll up to the count of ten. Do this exercise three times a week and you will start to see a powerful change.

SCENE 2

TELLING MORE STORIES

The global pop star Adele has released four albums to date, each named after her age when she wrote and released them:

- 19
- 21
- 25
- 30

The songs on those albums tell stories that only she could tell at that age – what it was like to be Adele at 19 is very different to Adele at 30. Each album defines an era.

Let's do the same with your story.

You have your Hero's Journey, your answer to the question, 'How did I get here?' Now, let's split it like a cell and see what other stories you can tell. The more you can tell the more you can weave into your world of work. Remember, these are stories that reveal something about you, your skill, your why, your motivation. They can be funny or sad. But every time you tell a story you engage on a profound level with your audience. They reveal your red thread, the stitching that goes all the way through you and makes you who you are.

If I were to choose four standalone stories, they would look like this:

- 13
- 18
- 21
- 32

When I was 13 Mr Stubbs stood me up in class.

When I was 18 I gave *that* school assembly.

When I was 21 I got into a theatre company that taught me everything I know and use today. When I was 32 Mia asked me to help her pitch and Amplify was born.

And there's more:

When I was 37 I had so badly damaged my ankle at a U2 gig in London that the next day, when I flew to Milan to do a job with Microsoft, I couldn't wear my shoes. I coached the entire two days in bright yellow and blue socks. Getting Milanese ice-cream late at night, barefoot, should be on everyone's bucket list...

Or, when I was 33 and took on my first official, paid job for Amplify, at Pentonville prison. I was told I would not at any point be left alone in a cell with a prisoner. But there I was, in a locked cell, just me and Stix – a six-foot-four guy who could have broken my arm with his little finger. He was about to be released and needed interview skills.

I mean, he really needed them.

I remember him slouching and looking at me like I had killed his cat, and me saying, 'Stix, if you want a job, you really need to smile.' I made it out with all my bones intact and he made it out with a smile.

Now it's over to you. If you can, give the Hero's Journey treatment to your chosen life 'moments', and turn each one into something between a 30-second anecdote and a two-and-a-half-minute story, then you will have a storytelling kit that will set you up for the future.

Write down four ages and four stories that you will transform with the Hero's Journey narrative.

1.

2.

3.

4.

SCENE 3

PRESENTING IN THE BUSINESS WORLD

In the US television series *Friends*, every one of the 236 episodes is entitled: 'The One With…' or 'The One Where…' You probably know some of them:

- 'The One With The Cop'
- 'The One With All The Cheesecakes'
- 'The One Where They All Turn 30'

...and so on.

Take a moment now to think about the next presentation you have coming up at work. Remember: a presentation could be a phone call with your line manager, a five-minute check in with your team, a meeting with your colleagues, or a job interview. We are going to turn this presentation into an episode of *Friends*. Here are some examples of what I mean:

- The one with the job interview
- The one with the weekly check-in where nobody speaks
- The one with the three-hour Zoom meeting
- The one where the family member keeps interrupting (not business-related, but just as real!)
- The one with the patronising colleague who thinks he should be paid more than me
- The one with the line manager who can't focus after lunch and is clearly distracted by something else

Write down your five 'episodes' here.

1. ....

....

2. ....

....

3. ....

....

4. ....

....

5.

Now it's time to get to work on your presentation. Bear in mind that you are not who you were when we started out on this journey. You are now a storytelling hero. You are on the road back. In fact, you have almost made it to the final act – Resurrection. Before we enter that promised land and reveal the stories you never thought you could tell, the presence and power you never thought you could embody, I would like to introduce you to another storytelling hero: here's Dan.

DAN STRANG

SERIAL ENTREPRENEUR

DITCHING THE JARGON

Dan is scrappy. He has been for as long as I have known him. He has this glint in his eye and a determination to create something out of any opportunity. That's what makes him a great entrepreneur. And I could see that back in 2012, when I was coaching him in a group workshop to pitch for the life of his company. He had the opportunity to get on the Wayra accelerator but was competing against other startups. His story was good but he had swallowed what I would call the 'jargon pill'. That's what happens when adrenaline kicks in, tells you that your story is not good enough and makes you feel like you have to be serious in order to convince people. But passionate Dan is so much more convincing than serious Dan.

I threw some tried-and-tested acting exercises at him, and coached him (somewhat brutally) to kill the jargon. He pitched, he won, and he went on to build Eventstag, raising over £2 million! It was an incredible journey – and then Covid hit. Once again, he had to fight for the life of his company and carry the weight of the future of his employees in the balance. Dan is a natural-born pitcher and, after much grit and grafting, Eventstag was acquired in late 2020. He posted the most beautiful LinkedIn post about it. Dan wears honesty well because now he knows how to tell a story. This is what he has to say in his own words about how storytelling has helped him throughout his career as an entrepreneur:

'When I was told I would get pitch coaching as part of the Wayra accelerator, I rather arrogantly thought, "I don't need that, I'm alright at pitching. I just need to work out all the other problems in my business." Five minutes with Stew and I realised I was no pitch pro (yet). He pulled my pitch apart and focused me on telling a story, bringing energy at the right moments and removing all the jargon. It worked and it helped me not only to win investment pitches but to win business and communicate better with my staff. Throughout the years, I've used Stew to help coach my sales teams, for friendly advice,

> and whenever I need some help with a big pitch. He's the best there is and – more than that – he's great to be around and always makes you laugh and enjoy the sessions.'

What did I do with Dan? We went through the first 30 seconds of his pitch and cleared it of jargon. So what can you learn from his story?

- Focus on presenting the first 30 seconds of your work presentation to a friend or trusted person who will be honest with you.
- Ask them to interrupt your pitch as soon as they start to switch off, or feel bored or confused. If they feel awkward about doing that, assure them that it will be your fault, not theirs!
- When they tell you it's not working, start the presentation again and try to focus on using picture, headline and detail.
- Don't assume you have nailed it! Allow your audience to let you know how it's going.
- Keep going until you can present for 30 seconds without them interrupting. If you get irritated, frustrated, or even angry at them then you are doing the exercise right! Anger is a great driver for good storytelling.

ACT V

RESURRECTION

SCENE 1

THE HERO'S JOURNEY, WITH A TWIST: CALLING YOUR AUDIENCE TO ACTION

Up to this point, you have been the hero on your own journey. But when it comes to bringing others with you – the goal of every single one of your presentations – you need to change gear. Now it's time to become something else, to step *beyond* the hero, so that you can empower others to be the hero of their own journey.

Delivering a business presentation in the role of the hero rarely goes well. We end up trying to prove our heroism to the audience. We defend ourselves and try to win approval. It is painful to watch and to listen to. We have all seen this and – probably – have all been guilty of it. Nobody enjoys a presentation where people are clearly trying to 'sell' them something. In this business story, you are no longer going to play the part of the hero.

It's time to become a wise mentor.

THE TRUCKING WISE MENTOR

Kuehne & Nagel are supply chain experts. You will see their name on the side of lorries up and down the country – and all around the world. They get goods from A to B. They founded Help Logistics because, in countries that need humanitarian aid, one of the biggest obstacles is the supply chains. There are no roads, no warehouses, no way of tracking the aid that is given. So Help Logistics use their expertise to build the infrastructure of their supply chains, to get food to famine-struck areas and aid to the most remote locations, so people can be fed, watered and looked after. In short: to save lives.

But they aren't the hero in this story.

In Kuehne & Nagel's Hero's Journey, they position the aid charities as the heroes and themselves as the wise mentor, to guide the hero along the way as they slay the dragon of broken roads and inadequate storage, so that people can be fed and lives can be saved.

And that is how they tell the story.

What about you?

Yoda never defends his Jedi identity. He is a Jedi, with or without Luke's approval.

Gandalf's ability to save the world doesn't depend on people believing him.

Haymitch has already won the Hunger Games and knows what it takes.

Morpheus lives in the real world and knows what freedom looks like.

If you are going to take your place as the wise mentor in the story, you must truly believe that you have a voice and that your genuine and authentic offering will help that person slay whatever dragon that stands between them and the treasure they seek. You have been on the journey and found your voice. You're ready, and you need to believe that.

Whether you are seeking promotion or a funding round, or whatever it may be, your identity as wise mentor remains the same. So how do you make sure that every time you deliver a presentation you do it with Yoda-mojo, Gandalf-confidence, Haymitch-knowledge and Morpheus-perspective? How do you steer clear of bad storytelling and adrenaline attacks? It starts with structure. Take a moment to think about your next presentation. Get your pen ready and answer the following questions.

Who is the hero/heroine (their name and the company name)?

....

....

....

What is the dragon they need to slay (what is their goal and what are the obstacles that stand in their way)?

....

....

....

What is the treasure they need to find? (Is it a new way of working, a new piece of tech, some customer insight?) This is the reason for your presentation – you have something that will help them.

....

....

....

How will you help them find their sword/inner strength (what is it about you that means only you can help them achieve this)? This is the meat of your presentation – offering a unique solution or insight that shows them that you are the person they need.

....

....

....

What will the promised land look like for them (personally, and for the business)? Paint a picture of what life will look like on the other side – it might be more profit, more possibility, more flexibility and freedom.

....

....

....

....

....

Now, take all of those answers and fill in six new bubbles, just like you did in your own Hero's Journey. Remember, now it's your audience that is the hero. Start by putting a catchphrase in each bubble to remind you of the section of the presentation you are covering.

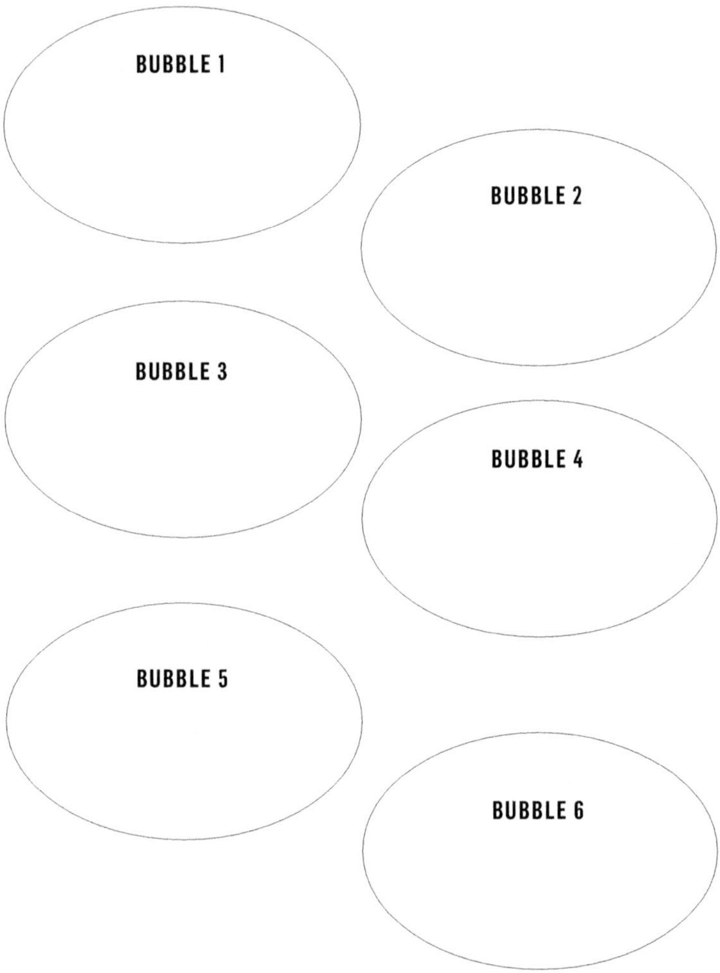

Now you have your bubbles it's time to present. As you present, remember you are the wise mentor and they are the hero.

Do it right now.

I dare you.

Start your own Zoom/Teams meeting or use my digital mirror. Just like you did before. Remember, adrenaline wants to take over. Don't let it. Just tell the story.

RECORD YOURSELF
AMPLIFY.ME.UK/MIRROR

SCENE 2

ROCKET FUEL EXERCISES: BRINGING ENERGY TO YOUR PRESENTATIONS

A bit like a riptide, there is a strong undercurrent of dull presentations in the business world, and it's all too easy to get swept up in it. The answer? Energy. As you go about telling the story of your business you will find yourself tempted to deliver a dead presentation. But here's the great news: it only takes two exercises to keep you energised and energising. But it does require you to attempt to present to seven-year-olds...

FROM KIDS' PRESENTER TO WHISPERER TO NEW NORMAL

I want you to deliver the first 30 seconds of your presentation as if you are presenting to kids. Every word has to be full of energy, and you're going to have to make some changes to the content because most kids don't get online platforms and stakeholder targets. Use big arms, big voice, and go all out!

Now deliver the next 30 seconds of your presentation in a whisper. Don't just pretend to whisper, or talk quietly. Actually whisper. Whisper it like it is the most sensitive secret in the world. Every word you say matters. Keep it secret.

Now go back and immediately deliver this one minute section again. Except, this time, you are delivering it as 'normal', or *new* normal. Hit record on your phone or laptop – trust me, you will want to see the difference for yourself. You will have absorbed both the energy of the kids' presenter and the intimacy of the whisperer into your body and voice. You are pumping full of energy and connection. As you deliver your new normal you will feel the flow – naturally, without trying. You might find different words flowing out unexpectedly, and you will be deeply, deeply engaging. I call this projected intimacy. You will draw your audience in by using your voice and body well.

PORTALS, PICTURES AND THE CURSE OF KNOWLEDGE

In Donald Miller's book *Building A StoryBrand* he talks about the curse of knowledge. When it comes to our own product, we are ten-out-of-ten on the knowledge scale. We know everything there is to know. And we tend to assume that our audience is about a six out of ten. In fact, you will tell a better and more engaging story if you assume that they are two out of ten.

The curse of knowledge is that we get lost in jargon. But if someone is two out of ten on your subject matter you're less likely to kick off your presentation this way. You will begin by trying to explain, to tell a story, to educate and inform. Even when working with people in the industry who do know the subject matter, I still tell my clients that it pays to assume they are two out of ten. Why? Because your audience has a brain. And, as we keep reminding ourselves, the brain is wired for picture. Your audience's brain just wants a picture. If you ignore that, you lose them.

I was once coaching a couple of Australians from a recruitment firm. They were trying to pitch their new job portal to their bosses, and this was their big opener:

'63% of clients said they needed a portal, where they can access all information in one place.'

When we framed it as a picture it changed to this:

'Imagine if every time you wanted to buy something from Amazon you had to send an email, wait for another email to confirm your purchase and then get on the phone to confirm

your order. You wouldn't buy from Amazon again. Our clients are experiencing this problem right now. But what they want is to be able to go onto one portal and have everything they need, right there.'

Could you feel the difference?

Take some time now to do exactly the same thing with your presentation, using the phrase 'Imagine if' as a prompt. Use the Amazon anecdote if it helps.

Here are some starter lines for you:

- Imagine if everyone in our organisation was fully engaged with every meeting.
- Imagine if we could track all of our customers' movements.
- Imagine if I told you that you could save 30 minutes a day.

Invite people to imagine! Using the phrase 'Imagine if' is a great catalyst for painting a picture.

Now go and get some more practice in. Find a willing audience and present to them. On-screen or off-screen. Channel the energy of the kids' presenter and the intimacy of the whisperer, choose storytelling and picture painting rather than a jargon dump, and watch them get swept up into your presentation.

SCENE 3

THE SILVER SCREEN: SHOWING UP ON CAMERA

Back in 2019 I was talking about this thing called 'Skype coaching' or 'video coaching' but nobody wanted it. In January 2020, I was coaching at Microsoft in Dublin, Ireland. We were introducing ourselves and someone in the room was trying to describe, with slight embarrassment, what they were working on. They mentioned this thing called 'Teams' and there was literally a snigger in the room. I asked what it was and they said 'It's the new Skype.' It was the embarrassing cousin at a wedding that nobody wants to talk to.

How things have changed.

Now, the embarrassing cousin is throwing their own wedding and we all want to be there. Now, people are realising that Covid is here to stay and so too is the screen. On one level it's amazing – you can speak to anyone, anywhere. Instant connection. In an interview with Harvard Business Review, Microsoft CEO Satya Nadella says he loves conducting meetings on Teams because he can click on someone's name and read their profile (a cool piece of Microsoft tech called Microsoft Viva). He can learn so much about a person before even meeting them. And then, if he wants to, he can request a 15-minute one-to-one meeting with them. Slightly terrifying![9]

But, on the other hand, we are all exhausted by being on screen all the time. We weren't designed to do life in isolation and to only have a flat screen to connect with. But this is the world we live in now. If people were already terrified of speaking in public, stopping them from interacting with people in real life and forcing them to engage with a computer screen will only compound that fear.

So, let's take that fear, that exhaustion, and turn it into an opportunity to learn the skills we need to make the screen work for us – not just to survive in this new, post-pandemic era, but to thrive. Here are seven tips that give you all the basics for showing up on screen every time. Take them to heart and they will transform your meetings.

1. **Have an online meeting with yourself to work out where your eyes need to be.** Spend a moment finding exactly where you need to look so that you're looking directly at people, and mark the spot with a small sticker (usually just underneath your camera).

2. **Anchor yourself to that spot as often as you can.** We naturally look at ourselves, but we need to look at other people to feel connected. Anchor your eyes, and when they drift away towards yourself, anchor again. Start by doing this every three minutes, then reduce the time gap until it becomes natural like breathing. It won't happen by accident. It happens only if you make it happen.
3. **Imagine an excited audience reaction to create energy.** Make your eyes alive by imagining that a person is directly behind your anchor spot or camera eye an that they are sitting on a sofa waiting for you to speak. They are excited to hear what you have to say. It will bring the sparkle and connection to your eyes that you need (especially if the people actually on screen are giving you no reaction and creating no energy!).
4. **Make sure that your camera is at least at eye-level.** Nobody enjoys staring up at people's nostrils, but we force people to do this all the time! They best framing for your face is where the camera eye is 15 degrees above your eyes. It is great for posture, frames your screen nicely and makes you easy to watch.
5. **Sit between 0.5m and 2m from your camera lens.** Too far away feels like you don't want to be in the meeting, and too close is just weird.
6. **Position a Post-it Note just above your screen to remind you of who you need to be.** We have so little

motivation from real physical interaction that we need to create our own energy and motivation. We need to have things that call us up to be the best versions of ourselves we can be. The screen can drain from us – these things can fill us up again.

7. **Smile, smile and then smile some more. Then keep smiling.** Only rarely to we see a Joker from Batman – an insane smile that freaks people out. But we see many faces of misery from people whose 'joy is so deep it hasn't reached their faces' (as my friend David Grant often says). Bring joy out of the depths and let it shine a bit more.

PRACTICE MAKES PERMANENT

My grandad had a stoop from when he worked in the mines. He never had physiotherapy to sort it out so eventually that stoop became part of his everyday walking, living and breathing. His body learnt to permanently stoop. But it could all have been different. This coaching we are doing is the physio my grandad never had. Let's imagine that you came to this book with a stoop that you were not aware of, or that you felt you had to live with. The great news is that you don't! If you want to, you no longer have to accept the stoop, to limp your way through a presentation. You can stand tall and unlock your voice.

As we get towards the closing scene of this epic journey into storytelling heroism, I invite you to spend some time with Anneka.

ANNEKA WALLINGTON

FOUNDER, RECOGNISED

PITCH WALKING

When I first met Anneka she had taken on the role of Marketing Manager for a charity. But it soon became clear that she had another passion – creating jewellery that was not only beautifully crafted but that also raised awareness of tough issues, such as cancer and mental health, and helped people feel recognised. She had a vision.

What was just a dream inside Anneka's head had to become a story that investors would get excited about. Investors can appear intimidating, but they were the audience she had to grab. And Anneka is a presence in a room. She has fire and passion and much to say. She is just built that way. It is who she is. But getting it out, allowing people to see the fire and not be overwhelmed by her strength of passion was her biggest challenge. Her problem was that she spoke at a thousand miles an hour. She would start telling a story but that story would get polluted with jargon and wouldn't land. She was finding it hard to see herself as the wise mentor.

So I took her for a pitch walk. There is something that happens when you have to walk and talk. All of the meaningless words fall out of your head and you are left with a terrifying creative space. Into that space, I started to draw out Anneka's story. I only let her speak in sentences that were short and free from jargon. Those two things could literally change a life. And it changed Anneka from someone whose passion is admirable to a businesswoman who knew how to tell the story of a dream, get funding to fuel that dream, and then build a business off the back of it. A businesswoman who did what she needed to do to help people who feel isolated and in pain find recognition and hope.

Today, Anneka's business Recognised is real, alive, online and in retail stores. Anneka was named Young Businesswoman of the Year by Santander in 2021, and one of the many ingredients to her success is that she knows who she is and she knows how to tell the story.

What can you take from Anneka's story?

One thing: take your business presentation out for a pitch walk, and walk and walk until you have it flowing through you. There is a rhythm to walking that will flow into your presentation and you will deliver it completely differently as a result of that. Get walking!

SCENE 4

THE CLOSING SCENE: REFLECTING ON YOUR STORYTELLING SKILLS

You've made it! You started this book in a very different place to where you are now.

You have learnt new skills, you have named and pulled out your gremlin, you have tamed the stallion of adrenaline, you have told your story like never before (maybe you have never before told your story), you have returned victorious, as a storytelling hero, and have taken these skills into the world of business – the future is so very bright! You have moved from hero to wise mentor. You are living with Gandalf's identity, Morpheus' freedom, Yoda's skills and Haymitch's wisdom! It's time to reflect on all you have done. I do this in my coaching sessions so I wanted to give this to you as our journey comes to a close.

In *The Inner Game of Tennis*, Timothy Gallway lifts the hood on tennis coaching: help them observe themselves and get them into the flow. It's time to sit back and observe yourself.

I would love for you to write down the top three things that you want to achieve in the next six months, all in the area of presenting and storytelling. It can be as specific as, 'I will speak in short sentences,' or as visionary as, 'I will always make my audience the hero.'

1. ....

....

2. ....

....

3. ....

....

One of the plus sides of working digitally is that no-one can see what's behind the camera. Try putting up these Post-it Note reminders so that you can see them while you're speaking or presenting. You can then ask yourself, after each call, where you succeeded and where you still have work to do – it's a great way to keep yourself accountable. These quick, 10-second reflections will keep you sharp.

THE NEW STANDARD

Let this be your new standard. Once you have this standard you have everything you need to speak freely. You will know if your voice is connected or if it is stuck in your throat. You will start to measure what 55% body language, 38% tonality and 7% text looks like. If you can feel it you can measure it, and if you can measure it you can own your own development. I have written this book to help you piece your stories back together so that they land with power and impact, empowering you to thrive.

And thrive I believe you will.

Earlier I said how listening transformed my business. How did it do that? It was August 2016. I was just about to head on holiday and was on an introductory call with Microsoft. We had spent 45 minutes talking about all things storytelling. It was all potential and, 'Maybe one day soon we will work together.' I suppose I was auditioning for the role of storytelling coach.

Right at the end of the call as I played back all I had heard, I said nine words that changed my life and the life of my family forever.

'Is there anything else you would like to add?'

To my complete surprise, the answer was: 'Actually, yes – we have a training event in Amsterdam in October. Can you deliver it? We will also have training in Barcelona, Switzerland, Spain and Portugal. And it all needs to be done before Christmas. Is that possible?'

Game.
Set.
Match.

I spent the next few months on the road and was able to set up my business for long-term success because of it. It led to more work which led to more work which led me to where I am today.

I have learnt over the years that if you listen well, people will want you to share. And if you listen at the end of what you share it shows that you actually care. It isn't just about the sound of your own voice. It's about the sound of collaboration.

In your storytelling, listen well, speak well, and repeat. Use those nine words. You never know what might happen!

You have crossed over the threshold of storytelling adventure, slain your dragon, arisen to the promised land and have become the wise mentor… Now it's time to speak! You are fully equipped to go boldly into the meeting rooms and boardrooms of your future.

And, talking of boardrooms, here is Steve to tell you how he overcame his gremlins and learned to speak with incredible confidence.

STEVE PIERCE

CHRO, HITACHI EUROPE

TRUSTING THE PROCESS

When you think Human Resources, I doubt you think, 'Oooh, exciting – bring on the popcorn!' More likely, you think of data, figures, salaries and admin. But there's nothing 'human' about that image of HR. Steve has been in HR for most of his career and suffered from the HR jargon problem – facts before story, three-letter acronyms before metaphors, abstract before detail. He knew that his story could be much more because the human story is so rich.

I first met Steve back in 2014, when he was preparing a 20-minute talk for an HR conference in his role as CHRO of Hitachi Europe. I asked him what he wanted out of it and he said that he was an experienced presenter but he wanted to learn how to become a great speaker and to raise the profile of Hitachi. He had leapt at the chance of speaking at this conference because he knew that emails alone don't cut it – there is power in speaking. Now, it was about getting the most out of this golden 20 minutes.

The facts themselves are less important than how you deliver them – he/she who tells the best story wins. Line by line, with both kindness and brutality, I corrected his breathing, raised his voice to be loud and impactful, and introduced a few eye-raising warm-up exercises – things you don't often see in the boardroom. But he embraced all of it and was relentless with his learning, because Steve is a voracious learner. This is what he had to say about it:

'We often use the term "lifelong learning", and some learning really can last a lifetime if it is relevant and impactful for our performance. Working with Stewart took me out of my comfort zone and gave me tools and techniques that I still always use for major presentations. It was hard work and challenging but has made a real difference, and presenting has become more enjoyable too!'

Just like Steve, I invite you to trust the process. Follow the exercises, practise and persevere, even when it feels weird and uncomfortable – *especially* then!

YOU'RE READY

Congratulations! Here we are at the end of your epic adventure. You have persevered, conquered, and returned home a storytelling hero. You know your story, and you've done the work to unlock your voice so that you can tell it with power and confidence. You carry a toolkit of skills and strengths that you didn't know you had (including listening, facilitating and networking). Now it's time to go forth, tell great stories and bring others on the journey with you by becoming their wise mentor. Maybe you have already started – I would absolutely love to know how this book has helped you. So please email me at stewart@amplify.me.uk to let me know how it's going, and to ask any questions that crop up.

But for now, let me send you on your way to unleash the power of your story. Storytelling hero, wise mentor – you're ready. It's what you were made to do.

EPILOGUE

FREQUENTLY ASKED QUESTIONS

At the end of my coaching sessions I always get asked some combination of the same questions. Below are the answers to these questions. I hope that in this final chapter of our adventure in storytelling, you will find the answers to any questions you have. If not, please do get in touch with me. From creating your content to delivering your story to listening well, I want you to be the best storyteller you can possibly be. It just makes all the difference.

WHAT DO I DO WITH MY ARMS?

Here is the secret – let them be! The only rule is not to force your hands to come together in front of you. If your hands are resting, without you giving them any thought, then they will rest at your sides. This frees people up to use them, or not use them, but there is no awkwardness here, no staged positions. The same is true when you are on the screen. Allow

ENERGY
AMPLIFY.ME.UK/ENERGY

your hands to rest on your lap or your table and use them whenever you want to. When they do go to rest, allow them to rest, separately, wherever feels most comfortable. That's it. The link on the left is a video on Energy to help with the common arm problem.

HOW DO I STOP PEOPLE FROM TALKING?

Sometimes you just have to interrupt, especially on the screen. It is awkward and painful but if you are losing the room it is better for one person to be offended (and they may well not be) than for the room to fall asleep. So I just say, 'Brian, I am going to have to ask you to draw this to a close / to round up what you're saying.' If he keeps going then you can say, 'Brian, we have one minute left.' When they stop, repeat back what they have said in the most concise way possible. This shows them that you listened, but also communicates to the room that you are in control.

PEOPLE SAY I AM TOO QUIET. HOW DO I FIX THAT?

Twenty years ago, I remember performing at an old people's home and they were blissfully unaware of what we were saying. Some of these wonderful old people would lean right in and were clearly on the verge of saying, 'Can you speak up dear? I can't hear.' Imagine you have a deaf granny sitting on the other side of the screen, who happens to hold the key to your business future. The only way she can unlock the door is if you speak loudly enough for her to hear, and make sure that the key points land! So over-pronounce your words. Do this for 30 seconds, be very deliberate, and then re-present with the new normal. Your voice will be clearer, and you will be intentional about the words you want to underline with your voice.

THIS BIT OF MY PRESENTATION IS BORING. HOW DO I FIX THAT?

There is an improvisation exercise that I would recommend, but it only works with a partner, so find someone who is willing to interrupt you and have fun! Give them permission to jump in at any point and say, 'That's great, tell me more about that.' For example, you say, 'In 2020 we went remote.' They say, 'Remote – that's great, tell me about that.' You have to tell the person about remote working as if they have never heard about it, so you have to use picture. You have to describe what the office used to look like, why people went to work in the first place (to earn money and look after their family) and what remote looks like (working from a computer). Whatever they ask you about, your challenge is to paint a clear picture for them and then get back on topic. This is not only fun – and frustrating! – but it highlights which of your words are full of meaning and picture, and which are not.

I KEEP FORGETTING WHAT I'M SAYING. HOW DO I FIX THAT?

It is usually when moving from one key point or section of a presentation to another that we can lose our way. We forget how we are going to start the next section so we get stuck. Often, we stumble on the same bit over and over again. If you do this three times on the same section, it's time to fix and not forget.

Here's the fix: create some great linking phrases that help you move smoothly from one section to the next. Speak aloud the last sentence of section one, the linking sentence, and the first sentence of section two. Repeat those sentences, over-pronouncing your words and making your face very big. Do this five times slowly, five times quicker, five times very fast, and then five times at normal pace. Then practise that bit of the speech. I learnt this at drama school and it works!

HOW DO I STOP MY HANDS FROM SHAKING OR MY FACE FROM SWEATING?

There are two exercises here that will feel counter-intuitive, but they will counter the adrenaline attack!

THE £1,000 A TICKET DINNER

Authority inspires confidence. If you are seated around a table with seven other people, all of whom have paid £1,000 to hear you speak, you will speak with confidence and authority. Your audience is here for you. Imagine this is the case with your real audience. Imagine they have paid £1,000 to hear you speak. Relax into it, be yourself, and take control of the content instead of the content taking control of you. Remember – people have paid a lot of money because they want to hear what you have to say!

THE COMEDIAN

Now re-tell a part of your presentation but imagine you are a comedian delivering a long build up to your killer joke. It will bring instant energy and personality to your words, and help you see which words don't matter. It will highlight picture, you will get into your flow, and you will be surprised at what you come out with. Remember it, write it down, and use it.

HOW DO I HANDLE AWKWARD SILENCES?

Tell the audience, 'I'm a big fan of awkward silences,' and then wait it out. If still no-one bites, call on someone. Warn them that you are going to do this, so that everyone knows there's a back up plan. This way, whether they answer voluntarily or you pick someone out, you have set the tone and are in control.

WHAT IF SOMEONE BLOCKS ME WHEN I ASK A QUESTION?

You ask a question and they block with a 'yes' or 'no'. Well, you have tried the best you can to listen, so now is the time to speak – put your proposal out there. If you are asking for money or approval for a project, they will have to react!

I HATE THE PERSON IN FRONT OF ME AND DISAGREE WITH WHAT THEY ARE SAYING.

This is why you playback. It keeps you calm, focused on them, and it enables you to see the world from their perspective. And that means that when you speak, they will be more ready to hear.

HOW DO I SHOOT A VIDEO AT HOME?

My friend Simon Baker produced a brilliant one-page document when my clients started asking to record on camera during lockdown, so I am not even going to try and re-word it. Here it is. This is everything you need to do to record yourself on a phone at home:

1. SHOOT IN LANDSCAPE (HORIZONTAL)

Turn your phone on its side!

2. GOOD SOUND IS CRUCIAL

Good sound is even more important than good picture. Choose somewhere quiet, with some soft furnishings and a carpet or rug to help minimise any echo.

3. LIGHT YOUR FACE

The more light you have, the better your image is going to be. The important thing is to light your face properly, preferably from slightly off to one side. You can use a window, but don't put your back to the window because you will end up as a silhouette.

4. CHOOSE A NICE BACKGROUND

Avoid using a background that's too cluttered, but it's okay to have things behind you in shot (e.g. your office). If you're using a blank wall, stand at least one metre in front of it to avoid any sharp shadows.

5. USE THE BACK CAMERA OF YOUR PHONE IF POSSIBLE

You'll get a better quality recording using the back camera of your phone – and not being able to see yourself on screen while you record might be less distracting too.

6. CHOOSE YOUR VIDEO RECORDING SETTINGS

Shoot at the highest resolution possible. Don't bother with a frame rate higher than 30, but 4K or 1080p (1920x1080) video is ideal. Don't choose a quality lower than 720p or 1280x720.

7. POSITION YOUR PHONE LEVEL WITH YOUR FACE

Position your phone at the same level as your face. If you find yourself looking up or looking down into the lens, you will need to reposition it. Use a tripod if you have one, or create a homemade one using a pile of books, a music stand or a stepladder.

8. FRAME YOUR SHOT CAREFULLY

Your eyes should be two thirds of the way up the screen. Your smartphone will give you a grid to help with this – go to Settings -> Camera -> Grid on iPhone or Camera -> Settings -> Grid lines on Android. The shot should include your head and at least your shoulders, but preferably a bit more of your body too.

9. TEST YOUR VIDEO RECORDING

Record a short test clip and check it carefully. When you've made an adjustment, record another test clip and check before you commit to your full presentation.

HOW DO I HANDLE A Q&A?

Imagine the questioner is handing you an energy baton, and when you receive it it's empty of energy. You have to charge it up. You do this by coming right out of the blocks and answering with incredible energy. If you need time to process, repeat the question back at them and check you have heard correctly. Then, use the question as a launchpad to tell a story.

That story will have the answer somewhere in it, but the main point is to employ this technique as you answer: pick up the energy, repeat the question, tell a story. You will then find your flow. Once you find your flow you will find you have confidence to answer the question.

I THINK I AM PRESENTING LIKE A NEWSREADER. CAN YOU FIX THAT?

Regularly, when watching my clients present, I will interrupt them, give a meaningful look, bring a pretend microphone to my mouth and say, 'And back to you in the studio…' If you sometimes sound like a newsreader, you're not alone. The problem is that newsreaders are reading off an autocue, so it can sound stilted and unnatural. They sometimes pause in the middle of sentences. They are speaking at you, not *to* you or *with* you, and they don't really care about you. To combat this, make sure you pause at the end of your sentences, not the beginning, and speak louder and faster. This will stop the 'slow read' effect. It works every time!

I HATE NETWORKING BUT I NEED TO DO IT. ANY TIPS?

Imagine that you are the MC of the night or the online event, and your job is to connect person A with person B. It is not about you and how awkward you feel. It starts with a fact-finding mission, and the assumption that everyone wants to be connected. You are a match-maker so when you meet people, choose to see this as a game. Ask a question like, 'What brought you here?' Then immediately playback what they have said so that your brain stores that information. Let the conversation flow or gradually wind down, then turn to the next person and ask them the same question. Repeat the same process, and then match make!

'So Fatima, you started life as an athlete and then went into IT, and John you actually started life in IT and now you are an avid table tennis player.' That's really all you need to do. The spark is lit and the conversation flows between John and Fatima. Without you, there would be no flow. People are far too self-conscious! You can stay in or move on. And if it doesn't flow – move on! No-one expects you to be their best friend.

HOW DO I HOST AN ONLINE MEETING ROOM?

Start with an exercise that everyone can do. Ask people what they had for breakfast and get them to put it in the chat. Then call on one person, repeat what they said, and say, 'Tell us about that.'

Or ask people to bring an object to talk about that means something to them. Tell them they will only have 30 seconds to present it. Then thank them. And, yes, you guessed it: play it back.

My friend Gibran asks people what their name means. That always gets people talking!

As you lead the meeting, speak in short, sharp sentences and move quickly from one item to the next on the agenda.

When you invite others to speak, address them by name. Sometimes, given the opportunity, they will inadvertently take the meeting between their teeth and jump into the river with it, like a dog with a stick. If this happens, don't panic. You can take control and get the meeting back. Playback what they said in 30 seconds to a minute, with great energy and enthusiasm (even if you have to fake it!), thank them and draw out one or two things that you see as being important to the meeting. Use this as a launch pad to move onto questions. This is crucial when someone has killed the energy in the room.

Be specific and direct when it comes to Q&A. If you just say, 'Any questions?' you are inviting a tumbleweed moment. You are the link between every question and answer. When someone asks or answers badly, play it back really well and swing to the next trapeze. You have the right to interrupt, at any time, so don't be afraid to do it. It is awkward but it is better to feel awkward than to lose 99% of your people. They will thank you for it.

Throughout the meeting, continually take a step back to summarise. At the end, be sure to round up what was said and what was agreed. Every time you do this you are giving people the opportunity to agree, disagree or add something more to the discussion. You are inviting connection and collaboration.

ACKNOWLEDGEMENTS

Carrie and David Grant – thank you for trusting me and showing me the power of coaching. We will always have Dubai! Mia Molinaro – you asked me to coach you and then paid for me to see the competition. It was enough to launch Amplify. James Stevenson – you were my first investor. Kim and Tim Verbrugge, you introduced me to LinkedIn and encouraged me every inch of the way in those early years. Paul Unsworth – you hired me as a barista and gave me a space to coach in. John Agnes – you were my first startup. Samit Patel – you were my second and opened wide the door to Google Campus and Alex Hawkes. Alex – you saw my first ever presentation on pitching and introduced me to Wayra and the world of accelerators. Ben Mumby-Croft, you were in the same talk, you said you'd do whatever you could to help me, and you have never stopped doing that! Jon Bradford, Diane Perlman, Belinda Raynes – thank you for taking a bet on me. Tom Chant – you have been a friend and mentor over all these years. Anu Pyysalo – you brought me to Microsoft and the rest of the world. Really, I am speechless. I will never forget the dancing in Dubai! Marcus Druen – thank you for helping me seal the deal with Microsoft and for coming along for the ride, life-changing for both of us. There are many, many others who I sadly can't mention here. But as I come into land: Steve Morris – your wisdom is nothing short of pure gold. Simon Baker – editor and friend, this book wouldn't be here without you. Thank you Finn and Zach Pile for recording the audiobook and Spike O'Connell at Runway East, Soho and Daniel Sanint at Flux Studios, Manhattan for production. Jose Raz Guzman – you changed the shape of this book for the better: thank you! And finally, Liz – words can never say what you mean to me. You are the ultimate champion of all I am and all I do. The hours you have spent sat with me at the kitchen counter (and often over a G&T) listening and listening and loving me through everything… thank you. I am so in love with you and it grows each day. I simply can't imagine Amplify without you.

NOTES

1 This phrase was coined by Jospeh Campbell. He wrote a book called *The Hero With a Thousand Faces*. You can read it but it is very long. Or you could read Jonah Sach's *Winning the Story Wars*. Or you could just take my word for it and go and find the Hero's Journey in every movie you watch!

2 She coined this phrase in her first ever TED talk, before she was famous. To date, 'The Power of Vulnerability' has over 58m views and this is the first thing she says. Watch it at https://www.ted.com/talks/brene_brown_the_power_of_vulnerability

3 Check out Dr Jennifer Aaker, General Atlantic Professor at Stanford Graduate School of Business, talking about this here: https://womensleadership.stanford.edu/stories

4 This excellent article from the University of Rochester will tell you more about the research that led to this fact: https://www.rochester.edu/pr/Review/V74N4/0402_brainscience.html

5 This is the basic premise of his book *Thinking, Fast and Slow*. The first three chapters will blow your mind!

6 It isn't just Donald Miller, but in his book *Building a StoryBrand* he talks about this as a key narrative technique. It's well worth a read.

7 And the charity, if you are interested, is Onelife – raising up a generation of young leaders for every sphere of society. Meet them at onelifeleaders.com.

8 You can find this and other tips in his book *Acting In Film*.

9 You can watch the whole interview here: https://www.youtube.com/watch?v=FRztx0wVuPA

Printed in Great Britain
by Amazon

83478365R00102